Also by Paul Begala

Is Our Children Learning?

Buck Up, Suck Up . . . and Come Back
When You Foul Up *(with James Carville)*

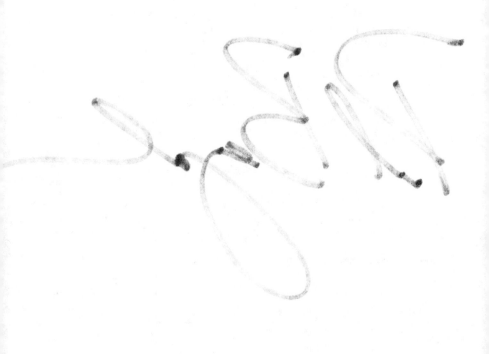

It's STILL the Economy, Stupid

★ ★ ★ ★ ★ ★

George W. Bush,
The GOP's CEO

PAUL BEGALA

SIMON & SCHUSTER
NEW YORK • LONDON • TORONTO • SYDNEY • SINGAPORE

SIMON & SCHUSTER
Rockefeller Center
1230 Avenue of the Americas
New York, NY 10020

SIMON & SCHUSTER and colophon are registered trademarks
of Simon & Schuster, Inc.

For information regarding special discounts for bulk purchases,
please contact Simon & Schuster Special Sales at
1-800-456-6798 or business@simonandschuster.com

Designed by Christine Weathersbee

Manufactured in the United States of America

10   9   8   7   6   5   4   3   2   1

Library of Congress Cataloging-in-Publication Data is available.

ISBN 0-7432-4647-0

Acknowledgments

The Democratic National Committee's research shop, under Jason Miner, is the best in the business. Jason and his team contributed immeasurably to this book by sharing with me their voluminous documentation of the economic wreckage of George W. Bush.

Dalit Toledano once again (as she did with my previous book) provided invaluable fact-checking, copyediting and creative input. Born in Israel, raised in New York, living in Venezuela—and soon (I hope) to be residing back here in America—Dalit is the best I've seen on any continent.

Jon Orszag, the Boy Genius of the Clinton economic team, was a constant source of facts, stats and encouragement, and his wife Rica was and is a delight in this and all projects. Peter Orszag (is it the DNA in that family that makes them so smart?) gave me focus and direction in discussing Social Security.

James Carville remains the best friend, partner and collaborator imaginable. His daily encouragement, focus and strategic insights shaped this book greatly (except, Mary, the parts you don't like. But then again, Mary's unlikely to like anything after this page).

I'd like to thank my good friends Mark and Susan Weiner for all their encouragement, friendship and support over the years.

There isn't a day that goes by that I don't check in with Rahm Emanuel, a font of good ideas and energy. He's going to be the most exciting thing to hit Congress since Preston Brooks caned Charles Sumner.

The gang from *Crossfire*—producers, crew, bookers and everyone else—was patient and supportive, and the cohosts on the right, Bob Novak and Tucker Carlson, did a better job of challenging my ideas and defending President Bush than Bush himself does.

David Rosenthal and Geoff Kloske of Simon & Schuster once again displayed tremendous faith in me, and in this book. They're quick, smart and tough. They would have made great campaign consultants; they're damn good publishers.

Bob Barnett, my attorney and friend (not, by the way, in that order), always provides sound advice and sage counsel.

Most of all, my family. Some of them share my politics; some of them don't, but all of them are extraordinarily supportive. My parents, David Begala and Peggy and Jerry Howard have always been a source of strength. My brothers—and their wives—David and Becky, Chris and Jeanie, as well as Mike, are always good for a laugh, an encouraging word and priceless real-world perspective. My sister Kathleen provides the advice, support and assistance that keeps me going. She is by far my favorite sister.

I hesitate to mention my in-laws, Dean and Jean Friday, Dave and Kate Friday, Bob and Leia Friday, and Ron and Terri Friday, since their Republican friends will likely ostracize them if their names appear in this book. But I can't resist.

My grandmother, Emma Begala, came to this country with nothing, built a family and gave them a future in the land of the free. She's taught us all about the American Dream.

Most important, today and every day, is my wife Diane. Through four kids, four moves, three books, two TV shows, countless campaigns, endless heartaches and thrills she has been true north—the most interesting, intelligent and moral person I've ever known. For twenty-one years, she's supported me financially when I was broke, bolstered me emotionally when I was down, challenged me intellectually when I was lazy and sustained me spiritually when I was spent. And it don't hurt that she's so damn easy on the eyes.

Our boys, John, Billy, Charlie and Patrick, are owed a special mention. They put up with a cranky and distracted daddy as I wrote this book. They give my life purpose.

Finally, to you, the reader. I have done my best to make this book as accurate as possible. Unlike many (indeed, most) political screeds, this is meticulously documented. Still, whatever errors may be here are my responsibility and mine alone.

For Bill and Hillary Clinton, Al and Tipper Gore, and all the people who made the Clinton administration's economic success a reality.

And, especially, for those courageous House and Senate Democrats who risked their careers (and in some cases, sacrificed their careers) to pass the Clinton economic plan into law.

Millions of Americans live better lives because of your service. Your work is more precious and more appreciated now that it's threatened.

CONTENTS

Introduction

When he campaigned for the presidency, George W. Bush promised Americans "prosperity with a purpose." Two years later, we have neither.

When he took office in 2001, George W. Bush inherited the strongest economy in American history. He inherited the largest federal budget surplus in American history—and the prospect of paying off the entire national debt in just eight years. He inherited a strong dollar and sound fiscal policy. He inherited a nation whose economy was so strong that commentators who, just a decade before, were predicting American decline were now complaining about American dominance.

And yet, Dubya blew it. Squandered everything he'd inherited from President Clinton.

We thought if Junior was good at anything it was inheriting things.

This is the story of how Bush blew it. How America's CEO—our first MBA president—has trashed our economy. How he wasted the surplus on massive tax cuts for the hyperrich. How he talked down the economy for his short-term political gain, then passed an economic program that has thus far put 1.8 million Americans out of work and cost investors $4.4 trillion. How he abandoned his free-trade rhetoric to adopt protectionist tariffs, effectively raising taxes on consumers. How he walked away from needed investments in education, training and all the things that make us smarter, safer and stronger economically. And how he plans to go on from here to cripple Social Security, and allow the privileged to avoid even more taxes.

If you read *Is Our Children Learning? The Case Against George W.*

Bush, you're probably thinking I'm going to say I told you so. I'm not. Bush himself told us so.

He always said he was going to run the country like a business. He just didn't tell us the business was Enron.

ONE

The Clinton Economy: "The Best Economy Ever"

"Mr. President . . . your commitment to fiscal discipline, which, as you know, and indeed have indicated, has been instrumental in achieving what in a few weeks . . . will be the longest economic expansion in the nation's history."—Alan Greenspan, Chairman of the Federal Reserve (1/4/00).

"The deficit has come down, and I give the Clinton Administration and President Clinton himself a lot of credit for that. [He] did something about it, fast."—Former Federal Reserve Chairman Paul Volcker, *Audacity* (Fall 1994).

"Clinton's 1993 budget cuts, which reduced red ink by more than $400 billion over five years, sparked a major drop in interest rates that helped boost investment in all the equipment and systems that brought forth the New Age economy of technological innovation and rising productivity."—*Business Week* (5/19/97).

"[This is] the best economy ever [because] on the policy side, trade, fiscal and monetary policies have been excellent, working in ways that have facilitated growth without inflation. The Clinton Administration has worked to liberalize trade and has

used any revenue windfalls to reduce the federal budget
deficit."—Goldman, Sachs & Co. (March 1998).

"I believe this will lead to a recession next year. This is the
Democrat Machine's recession, and each one of them will be
held personally accountable."—Rep. Newt Gingrich (R-GA)
Republican press conference (8/5/93).

WHEN MY GRANDMA BEGALA TELLS MY KIDS STORIES ABOUT THE
Great Depression—one in four working people unemployed, bread
lines and soup lines stretching around the block, rich men jumping
out of windows and poor men living on the streets—it is literally
impossible for me to imagine just how bad things were. They were
that bad.

I fear that when I'm in my eighties, telling my great-
grandchildren about the Clinton economy, it may be impossible for
them to imagine just how good times were. They were that good.

And, even though it's only been two years, memories fade. The
Republican blame machine has been working overtime, hammering
away relentlessly at America's accomplishments, hoping you'll forget the winning ways and broad prosperity of the Clinton Era.
They'd like to convince us that our nation was never that strong,
never all that smart, never that successful.

And yet, we were. As Casey Stengel used to say, "You could look
it up."

So, let's look it up.

Jobs

The heart of any economy is its ability to generate jobs. When President Clinton took office, nearly 10 million Americans were unemployed.[1] And the private sector was sputtering to create jobs—in
fact, during the previous Bush presidency, what little job growth we
did see was driven in large part by the government sector. Under
President Clinton, by contrast, the American economy generated
22.88 million new jobs.[2] More jobs than had ever before been created
under a single administration.[3] More jobs than Presidents Reagan

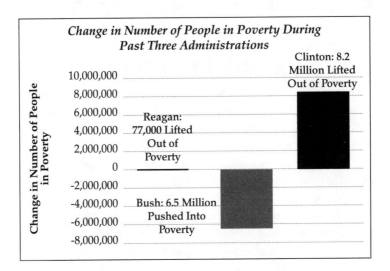

and Bush Senior together created in twelve years.[4] And 91 percent of the Clinton jobs were in the private sector.[5]

Poverty

If generating jobs is the heart of an economy, reducing poverty is its soul. We've had periods of macroeconomic growth that had very little effect on poverty rates. That's because all the benefits of the growth went to a few people at the top of the economic pyramid. Such was the case during the Reagan years. During Reagan's entire presidency, only 77,000 Americans were lifted out of poverty.[6] Not even enough to sell out Royal-Texas Memorial Stadium for a Texas Longhorn football game.[7] A paltry 0.24 percent reduction in the poverty rate.[8] Pathetic.

Under President Clinton's economic policies, 8.2 million Americans were lifted out of poverty.[9] Enough to populate all of New York City.[10] President Clinton's economic policies caused a 21 percent reduction in the poverty rate—the greatest reduction since Lyndon Johnson's Great Society and the strong economy of the 1960s.[11]

(By the way, under George Herbert Hoover . . . err . . . Walker . . .

The Poor Will Always Be with You (Especially When the Republicans Are in Power)

Jesus said "you always have the poor with you."[12] I fear some Republicans take that as an excuse to do nothing about the problem of persistent poverty. Think I'm overstating it when I say too many Republicans are too callous about the plight of the poverty stricken? Read this *New York Times* coverage of President George Herbert Walker Bush's strategy to deal with poverty in 1990:

"After considering a variety of ambitious options, the Bush administration has decided against proposing any major new program or strategy to combat poverty at this time, administration officials said today. An interagency group, convened last year by a senior adviser to President Bush to rethink the nation's anti-poverty efforts, came up with a dozen broad alternatives. But in meetings over the last two weeks, a higher-ranking group, the President's Domestic Policy Council, decided that the options were too expensive or would stir too much political controversy. The council, a Cabinet-level advisory board, concluded that the administration should simply try to make current programs work better. A White House official summarized the upshot this way: 'Keep playing with the same toys. But let's paint them a little shinier' . . .

"The White House acknowledged that a major new 'investment in children' would have a big payoff for American society in the long run, but it shelved the idea after concluding that it was 'not likely to show an immediate reward.' . . . Although administration officials could not agree on specific proposals to reduce poverty, they did agree on a theme to link existing programs. The message, as described in papers circulated among Cabinet members, is . . . 'economic empowerment' for American families."[13]

Bush, the number of Americans suffering in poverty *increased* by 6.5 million.[14])

Why the disparity? It's the difference between a temporary boom for a few, and sustained prosperity for many—what John F. Kennedy called "a rising tide (that) lifts all boats."

And lift all boats the Clinton economy did. Both the African-American and Hispanic poverty rates fell to their lowest levels on record.[15] The number of African-American children in poverty fell nearly 33 percent, to an all-time low.[16]

Child poverty was the most shameful and painful measure of our economic performance in our past. President Clinton attacked this persistent problem and made more progress than anyone thought possible. His policies reduced poverty among children by almost 30 percent—the biggest decline since the '60s.[17] President Clinton raised 4.2 million children out of poverty.[18] President Reagan, on the other hand, championed policies that focused on the fortunate few. His administration lifted only 50,000 kids above the poverty line.[19] We still have a long way to go before we can honestly say that no child has been left behind. Of course, if poor kids could eat speeches, Dubya would have fed the world by now. But his abandonment of President Clinton's focus on child poverty will haunt us for years to come.

Lifting All Boats

Under President Clinton, the typical American family's income increased by $7,418 after adjusting for inflation.[20] This is more than twice the increase in income during the Reagan–Bush years.[21] In fact, as Gene Sperling, the brilliant chairman of the National Economic Council under President Clinton has documented, "during the Reagan–Bush era, 60 percent of households had no gains in income—and the bottom 20 percent saw incomes decline 4 percent."[22]

During the Reagan–Bush era, the richest 20 percent of families saw their incomes rise dramatically, while the poorest families fell further and further behind.[23] By contrast, in the Clinton era, every income group, from the richest to the poorest, saw income gains of at least 15 percent, adjusted for inflation, and the poorest 20 percent of families experienced the largest income gains—24 percent in real terms.[24]

The income of the typical African-American family increased a remarkable $8,854, or 35 percent, after accounting for the effects of inflation.[25] And the gains made by those with the most ground to cover were the most striking. Consider this: from 1981 to 1992, the poorest 40 percent of African-American families saw their incomes fall by an average of 10 percent; during the Clinton administration, those same African-American families saw their incomes rise by an amazing 51 percent.[26]

For Hispanic families, the difference between the 1980s and the 1990s was similar: between 1981 and 1992, the poorest 80 percent of Hispanic households saw their incomes drop by an average of 6.7 percent; during the Clinton administration, the poorest 80 percent of Hispanic families experienced an average income increase of 25 percent.[27]

So, never again wonder why Bill Clinton is so beloved by the poor, by African-Americans and by Hispanic-Americans. It's because his policies helped them live the American Dream—a dream that had been nothing more than the stuff of pious, pompous lectures under the Republicans.

Taxes: Higher on the Idle Rich; Lower on the Working Poor

When it came to taxes, President Clinton's ideas were not new. They were as old as the biblical invocation that "From everyone who has been given much, much will be required."[28]

President Clinton's 1993 economic recovery package included an increase in the top marginal rate from 31 percent to 39.6 percent, which applied only to income above $250,000 a year. It also called for an increase in the federal gas tax of less than a nickel, and subjected the Social Security benefits of high-income retirees (whose average wealth was in excess of $1 million) to taxation.

Even as he raised taxes—primarily on the very rich—Clinton cut taxes deeply for the working poor. He greatly expanded the Earned Income Tax Credit—a tax incentive that rewards low-income people for working. Ronald Reagan signed the first EITC bill into law. President Clinton expanded it to make 15 million low-wage working families eligible. Combined with an increase in the minimum wage (from $4.25 to $5.15 an hour), Bill Clinton did more to reward, encourage and sustain low-wage working men and women than any president in history.

This was followed by a middle-class tax cut, signed into law in

1997. That law created a $500 per child tax credit, which, when combined with the Earned Income Tax Credit, meant that most middle-class and lower-income Americans had received real and meaningful tax cuts from President Clinton—even as we eliminated the deficit.

The Deficit and the Debt

When Bill Clinton was elected president, the deficit was the highest in history—$290 billion per year.[29] In fact, in January 1993, the Congressional Budget Office projected that, in the year 2000, the annual federal budget deficit would be $455 billion, and reach a staggering, crushing, astronomical, economy-choking $653 billion in 2003.[30]

These projections may have been good mathematics, but they didn't take into account the political will that President Clinton, Vice President Gore, and the House and Senate Democrats summoned to address the fiscal crisis.

Bill Clinton promised, above all, hope. And he delivered it in abundance. Shortly after Clinton took office, the *Financial Times* wrote, "The market opened markedly higher as investors and dealers got their first chance to react to Sunday's comments by Mr. Lloyd Bentsen, the new treasury secretary, which suggested the White House views cutting the deficit as a top priority."[31]

And the *Wall Street Journal*, just days after the president announced his economic recovery package, reported, "The spectacular bond market rally accelerated yesterday, with long-term Treasury bond yields plunging to another record low as investors rushed to embrace President Clinton's economic package."

By taking on the budget deficit—which Ronald Reagan once dismissed as "big enough to take care of itself"—President Clinton restored faith in America's fiscal policy. His policies freed up funds for private investment by reducing the *deficit premium*, the increase in interest rates caused by the federal government's borrowing (which crowded out private borrowers). This in turn unleashed a wave of investment and productivity that spurred the long-term, broad-based economic strength of the Clinton era.

Investing in People

Clintonomics was about more than fiscal policy. As the private sector was investing in new plants and equipment, technology and infrastructure, the government was investing in an even more precious resource: people.

President Clinton's budgets were designed to help people make the most of the new opportunities, with a heavy emphasis on education. He made the largest single investment in higher education since the GI Bill: doubling financial aid by greatly expanding Pell Grants, increasing the availability and affordability of student loans and work-study programs, establishing Educational IRAs and creating the Hope Scholarship and Lifetime Learning tax credits for college. Clinton also increased investments in education technology, charter schools, Head Start and other education programs. He created a welfare-to-work tax credit that encouraged employers to hire long-term welfare recipients, and assisted communities in moving welfare recipients into lasting, unsubsidized jobs. His Gear-Up initiative helped 700,000 low-income, middle-school students prepare for college, and 150,000 more have saved for college by serving their country in AmeriCorps.[32]

In 1994, President Clinton signed legislation creating Early Head Start for early childhood development, which helps ensure that kids begin school ready to learn. And, for adults who feared being left behind in the New Economy, Clinton nearly tripled resources for dislocated workers through his Universal Re-employment Initiative, and reformed the nation's patchwork system of job training by setting up one-stop job centers under the Workforce Reinvestment Act of 1998.

Creating Jobs by Expanding Trade

Clinton believed firmly that, as a country with only 4 percent of the world's population, but 20 percent of its productive capacity, America had no choice but to embrace free trade. We needed the overseas markets, and, he often noted, with all of the world's countries and cultures represented among our citizens, the United States was the best-positioned nation on earth to master globalization.

Even though the Republican Congress refused to grant him Fast-Track Trade Promotion Authority, President Clinton negotiated nearly 300 free and fair trade agreements. And, during his presidency, U.S. exports of goods and services grew by 72 percent—to top $1 trillion for the first time.[33] Exports alone supported 1.4 million new American jobs—jobs that paid as much as 16 percent above the national average.

Clinton's commitment to free trade caused him an enormous amount of pain from some of his best friends and strongest supporters. Trade has long been an issue that divides Democrats, but Clinton would not budge from his commitment to free trade. He angered unions and many loyal Democrats by fighting for passage of the North American Free Trade Agreement (NAFTA) in 1993. He won approval of Permanent Normal Trade Relations with the People's Republic of China—another issue that cost him dearly among his fellow Democrats. He successfully completed the Uruguay Round of free trade talks, fought for the first-ever African and Caribbean Basin trade bills, and dramatically expanded efforts to fight child labor and expand basic education around the world.

Despite the enormous pressure from his friends and supporters in organized labor, Clinton resisted protectionist tariffs on imported steel. As his political adviser, I thought the call was easy; helping steelworkers is smart politics. But Clinton knew that tariffs would do more damage than good, might set off retaliatory taxes on American goods, and do nothing to address the fundamental problems in the steel sector. So Clinton refused steel protectionism. His Republican successor, as we shall see, was neither as strong nor as principled.

Opening Markets at Home

Clinton brought the same zeal he showed in promoting American goods and services overseas to his quest to revitalize the inner cities. He created Empowerment Zones to spur local community planning and economic growth in distressed communities through tax incentives and federal investment. Thirty-one Empowerment Zones and 95 Enterprise Communities leveraged over $10 billion in new private sector investment, creating thousands of new jobs. He also sought to put the capital back in capitalism by creating Community Development Financial Institutions, which loan money to small businesses in the inner city. He embarked on what he called "new markets trips" to inner cities and Native-American tribal lands—bringing corporate executives and investors with him in much the same way that presidents and cabinet officials had traditionally brought American investors to explore new markets overseas.

Clinton also strengthened the Community Reinvestment Act, which encourages big banks to lend money to hard-pressed areas. According to the National Community Reinvestment Coalition, the Community Reinvestment Act has spurred more than $1 trillion in financial commitments to low- and moderate-income borrowers and neighborhoods—and 98 percent of those commitments occurred on President Clinton's watch.[34]

Reducing the Size of the Federal Government

Clinton did all this—and more—while reducing the federal workforce by 270,000 positions. So, the next time some right-wing government hater says Clinton was a big-government liberal, you tell him or her that Bill Clinton presided over the smallest federal workforce—in absolute numbers, not even adjusted for population size or anything else—since John F. Kennedy.

Clinton—with enormous help from Al Gore—reinvented the federal government, making it leaner and more effective than it had been in a generation. Government spending as a share of the economy, 21.2 percent under Bush Senior, was cut to just 18 percent—the lowest level since 1966.

Right-Wing Myths about the Clinton Prosperity

1. "It'll never work." The surest proof that the Clinton economic recovery plan represented a complete rejection of Reaganomics is the viciousness with which it was attacked by the Republicans. Here are just a few of the naysayers' comments from 1993:

- "I believe this will lead to a recession next year. This is the Democrat Machine's recession, and each one of them will be held personally accountable." Rep. Newt Gingrich (R-GA)[35]
- "We are buying a one-way ticket to a recession." Sen. Phil Gramm (R-TX)
- "It's like a snakebite. The venom is going to be injected into the body of this economy; in our judgment it's going to spread throughout the body and it's going to begin to kill the jobs that Americans have." Rep. John Kasich (R-OH)[36]
- "I really do not think it takes a rocket scientist to know this bill will cost jobs." Sen. Charles Grassley (R-IA)[37]

- "It is going to hurt the economy dramatically. They are going to do irreparable harm to this economy." Rep. Dan Burton (R-IN)[38]
- "April Fool, America. This Clinton budget plan will not create jobs, will not grow the economy, and will not reduce the deficit." Sen. Pete Domenici (R-NM)[39]
- The Clinton plan "will grow the government and shrink the economy. It will mean fewer jobs for ordinary Americans." Rep. Dick Armey (R-TX)[40]

2. "Reagan's policies created Clinton's boom." This one's funny, until you think about it. Then you realize it's pathetic. Reagan's economic policies jacked up the deficit, quadrupled the debt, and left us tens of billions of dollars of interest payments for years to come. Besides, if Reagan's economic policies were so impervious to Clinton's reforms, why did the Republicans so bitterly attack Clinton's proposals?

3. "The expansion really started under George Bush Senior." The official date of the birth of the expansion is March 1991, but 1991 and 1992 were years of anemic economic growth, which is one of the reasons the American people booted Bush out of office. In March 1991 unemployment was 6.8 percent. By June 1992, it was 7.8 percent.[41] Hardly a sign of a healthy economy. Here's what the experts were saying at the time:

- "The economy is comatose and shows only the faintest signs of life right now." Bruce Steinberg, economist, Merrill Lynch, *Washington Post* (9/26/92)
- "There are real signs here that the economy is sliding badly, surprisingly badly." Alan Sinai, chief economist, Boston Co., *Washington Post* (9/26/92)
- "Americans have been unable to mount a convincing economic recovery ... the economy is crawling forward so slowly that it appears to be standing still." Steve Mufson and John Berry, *Washington Post* (9/10/92)
- "First came the recession, which began in July '90 and seemed to end in early '91. Then there was the disappointing

stall the second half of last year—not another recession, but enough of a slowdown in sales and rise in unemployment to get people talking about a double-dip economy. Now there are rumblings of a triple-dip." Mark Memmot, *USA Today* (7/23/92)

- "The most recent economic news points to the possibility that the country may be heading for a triple-dip recession. Historians may look back on the Bush presidency as the beginning of a Great Recession, a period of prolonged economic stagnation." Charles Krauthammer, *Chicago Sun-Times* (7/12/92)

4. "It WAS Bill and Al—Bill Gates and Alan Greenspan." While no one can doubt Bill Gates's business acumen or Alan Greenspan's unparalleled genius as a central banker, the hard truth is that they were still on the job as Dubya plunged us into another Bush recession. Presidents matter and their economic policies matter. Just ask Chairman Greenspan:

- "President Clinton said to Chairman Greenspan, 'I have to congratulate you. You've done a great job . . .' 'Mr. President,' Greenspan replied, 'I couldn't have done it without what you did on deficit reduction. If you had not turned the fiscal situation around, we couldn't have had the kind of monetary policy we've had.'" *Maestro: Greenspan's Fed and the American Boom* (Bob Woodward, 2000)
- In his public statement when he was renominated to chair the Fed, Greenspan said to President Clinton, "My colleagues and I have been very appreciative of your support of the Fed over the years, and your commitment to fiscal discipline, which . . . has been instrumental in achieving what in a few weeks . . . will be the longest economic expansion in the nation's history."[42]

The Bottom Line

I hope this chapter didn't feel like trying to take a drink of water from a fire hose. But when you get a die-hard Clintonista—or anyone else with a command of the facts—on the subject of Clinton and the economy, well, the facts and stats just come gushing out.

It is beyond dispute that Bill Clinton was the most successful president on economic policy since Franklin Delano Roosevelt. The Clinton years brought the longest, strongest, broadest, fairest economic expansion in American history. Clinton didn't get a short-term jolt by running up the deficit, like Reagan. He didn't throw up his hands like Bush Senior. And he didn't allow our nation's economic fate to be determined by lobbyists and looters like Dubya.

Clinton followed the title of his campaign book, *Putting People First.*

It is staggering to observe the damage George W. Bush has done to our economy in just two short years.

But the purpose of this book is to prod policymakers—and voters—into demanding change, simply by chronicling the wreckage.

TWO

Tax Cuts for the Rich;
Deficits for the Rest

"If we do our job right and don't burden the economy with old quick fixes that have appeal, like enormous tax cuts that can't be paid for, I think things will come around."—Wisdom from the man our current president calls "Poppy" or "41"—then-President George H. W. Bush.[1]

"A tax cut is really one of the anecdotes to coming out of an economic illness."—George W. Bush (*The Edge with Paula Zahn*, 9/22/00).

"The Bush tax cuts benefit all Americans, but reserve the greatest percentage reduction for the lowest income families."—George W. Bush's campaign, announcing its tax cut proposal, 12/1/99. ("Governor George W. Bush: A Tax Cut with a Purpose") 12/1/99, available online at http://www.taxplanet.com/bushfactsheet.pdf.

"Nationwide, an estimated 12.2 million low- and moderate-income families with children—31.5 percent of all families with children—would not receive any tax reduction from the Bush [tax cut] proposal."—Center for Budget and Policy Priorities (CBPP Fact Sheet, http://www.cbpp.org/3-6-01tax.htm, 3/6/01).

"Governor Bush's tax cuts will be financed exclusively out of the non-Social Security surplus."—George W. Bush's campaign, announcing its tax cut proposal, 12/1/99.[2]

"Contrary to campaign pledges to wall off the Social Security trust fund from other uses, Mr. Bush proposes using all the Social Security surpluses—and then borrowing from the general public beyond that—to fund the government for the next two years, and to spend well over $100 billion of Social Security funds in each of the following three years."—*Wall Street Journal* (2/5/02).

ON THE CAMPAIGN TRAIL IN 2000, GEORGE W. BUSH PROMISED THE American people we could have it all. He said he could cut taxes, balance the budget, pay down the national debt, increase spending on defense, save Social Security (and create private accounts for young people saving to retire), all while boosting spending on education and helping seniors pay for prescription drugs.

When Al Gore, nudge that he is, pointed out that all of those promises came with price tags and that Bush's numbers didn't add up, Dubya accused Gore of "fuzzy math." Rather than do the math themselves, the media behaved like high-school kids who'd rather join the rich and popular kid in mocking the brainiac. Few held Bush's feet to the fiscal fire.

So, Bush became president (due to a little fuzzy math in the Florida vote count). When he was inaugurated, the federal budget showed a surplus for the year 2001 of $281 billion—the largest in American history. The ten-year surplus was projected to be $5.6 *trillion*. (Yes, trillion.) We were on track to completely eliminate the national debt by 2009.[3] And the Social Security system was racking up tidy surpluses, to be used when the baby boomers retire.

Today, all that annual budget surplus is gone. Even the Bush White House admits to a budget deficit this year of $165 billion.[4] The Center on Budget and Policy Priorities called this meltdown "the biggest one-year deterioration in projected budgets since 1982, following enactment of the Reagan tax cut in 1981."[5] And Republicans on the Senate Budget Committee acknowledge that things are only getting worse: They are predicting that the deficit will grow to $200 billion in 2003.[6]

What's more, the ten-year surplus estimate, which was $5.6 trillion when Bush took office, has dropped by $5.3 trillion.[7] Let me be clear. This isn't a typo. It hasn't dropped *to* $5.3 trillion. It's dropped *by* $5.3 trillion. A 94 percent reduction.[8]

Five-point-three trillion dollars of our surplus is gone. Vanished. Vaporized. That's a lot of money to piss away—even for a trust-fund baby like Junior. To put it into perspective, $5.3 trillion is enough to buy *two* new Jaguar X–Type luxury sedans for every family in America,[9] plus a hundred bottles of vintage Dom Perignon champagne for every American family,[10] plus four pounds of exotic, expensive Beluga caviar from Russia.[11] And still have enough money left over for eighty-two jars of Grey Poupon mustard.[12]

Rather than drowning you in luxury goods—or more realistically, eliminating the national debt in a decade, Bush has been forced to ask Congress to raise the debt ceiling by $750 billion.[13] And the Social Security Trust Fund is being raided—and will be raided every year until at least 2012, draining $1.97 trillion from the funds we need to support the baby boomers' retirement.[14]

How did we get into this mess? Or, rather, how did Dubya get us into this mess? The answer is simple: Ideas have consequences. Policies matter. Presidents matter.

And math is not fuzzy.

To his credit as a politician, Bush was able to persuade Congress to enact his massive tax cut for the rich. To the eternal shame of the Democrats, one-fourth of the Senate's Democrats went along with the plan. However, in passing his tax cut, Bush did not repeal the laws of mathematics—the inexorable reality that sucking $5.3 trillion out of the fiscal picture leaves one hell of a hole.

Hey, George: Where'd the Money Go?

According to an analysis of the Bush tax cut by Citizens for Tax Justice (CTJ), 37.6 percent of the Bush tax cut goes to the top 1 percent of wage earners. The Congressional Budget Office (CBO) estimated that the tax cut will cost more than $1.7 trillion over ten years.[15] The Bush tax cuts for the wealthiest 1 percent—only the wealthiest 1 percent of us, mind you—cost $507.6 billion over the next ten years.[16]

To put that into perspective, Bush's tax cut gives the richest 1 percent one-and-a-half times more money than the entire budget of the Department of Education, and more than the entire budget of the Department of Veterans Affairs or the Department of Transportation, and nearly nine times more than the entire budget for the Environmental Protection Agency.[17] And that's just the portion that goes to the wealthiest 1 percent.

What could we have done with that money? Plenty. How about saving Social Security, as President Clinton suggested? An analysis done by the brilliant economist Peter Orszag, for the Center on Budget and Policy Priorities, found that over the next 75 years the Bush tax cut will cost twice as much as the Social Security shortfall. During this time frame the Social Security shortfall is expected to be 0.72 percent of GDP or $3.7 trillion in present dollars. By comparison, the Bush tax cut, if extended, will cost 1.68 percent of GDP, or $8.7 trillion in present dollars.[18] We could have guaranteed that there would be no cuts in Social Security until the last baby boomer draws his last breath, and still have had $5 trillion left over for other pressing needs, like education, homeland defense and health care.

Of course, that overfed, overprivileged 1 percent may not be very many people, but they're Bush's people, and you gotta admire how well he takes care of them. According to the Citizens for Tax Justice, under the Bush tax cut, the wealthiest 1 percent of taxpayers would receive an average of $53,123 per year—$1,021 a week—in tax cuts.[19] That's more in tax cuts alone each year than most families earn in their total income in a year. Think about it. If you're a middle-class family, you're working, your spouse is working. You're missing Little League games and dance recitals to earn the money you need to support your family. And some rich dilettante gets a check from the government for $53,123—more than you get from your employer for busting your butt, while he's sitting on his? No wonder why Bush is the poster boy of the idle rich.

If you're at the other end of the wage scale, earning less than $15,000 a year, your tax cut averages $1.27 a week. A buck twenty-seven a week. Don't spend it all in one place.[20]

Middle-income taxpayers don't fare much better. On average, the middle 20 percent of wage earners, those who earn between $27,000 and $44,000, would receive $11.54 a week in tax cuts.[21] A couple of six-packs of beer.

Cheers.

Even a couple of six-packs is better than what 12.2 million American families were slated to get in Bush's original tax cut proposal. According to an analysis by the Center on Budget and Policy Priorities, "Nationwide, an estimated 12.2 million low- and moderate-income families with children—31.5 percent of all families with children— would not receive any tax reduction from the Bush proposal. Approximately 24.1 million children—33.5 percent of all children—live in the excluded families. The vast majority of the excluded families include workers."[22]

Under the Bush tax plan, as it was presented to Congress, 3 million African-American families with children would receive no benefits. That's 52.8 percent of all black families with children.[23] Hispanic families didn't fare any better. Three million Hispanic families with children—52.9 percent of all Hispanic families with children—would receive no benefits.[24]

How can this be? Didn't Bush promise to cut taxes for all Americans? According to the Center on Budget and Policy Priorities, these families are eliminated because they "have incomes too low to owe federal *income* taxes; the Bush plan cuts only income taxes and taxes on large estates."[25] The Bushies argue that it's hard to give a tax cut to people who don't pay taxes. Ahh, but they *do* pay taxes. They pay all kinds of taxes. They pay payroll taxes, sales taxes, excise taxes, gas taxes, property taxes and more, but Bush didn't propose to cut any of those taxes. He carefully targeted the taxes that rich people pay: income and estate taxes.

Bush's Tax Cut Caused the Deficits

One of the myths the Bushies have tried to spread is that the skyrocketing deficit was not caused by the Bush tax cut for the rich—as if handing hundreds of billions of dollars to the megarich could be done without any fiscal consequences.

In January 2002 the Congressional Budget Office found that the Bush tax cut was the largest single factor for the declining surplus. "As an illustration of how quickly the budget outlook can change," CBO's director testified, "CBO's projection of the cumulative surplus for 2002 through 2011 has plunged by $4 trillion in just one year . . . some $2.4 trillion of that drop can be attributed to legislative actions. *The legislation with the largest effect was the Economic Growth and Tax Relief Reconciliation Act of 2001,* enacted in June," CBO said. (Emphasis added.)[26]

The Center on Budget and Policy Priorities concurs: "The [January 2002] CBO figures also show that the tax cut of last June is the largest single factor in the ten-year, $4.0 trillion deterioration of the surplus, accounting for 41 percent of it," CBPP said. During testimony before the Senate Budget Committee, CBO Director Dan Crippen was directly asked if the Bush tax cut accounted for almost 42 percent of the loss of the surplus. "Yes," replied Crippen.[27]

Of course, massive deficits are not what Dubya promised. He said we could have it all. In a speech at Western Michigan University, he told us, "Tax relief is central to my plan to encourage economic growth, and *we can proceed with tax relief without fear of budget deficits, even if the economy softens.*" (Emphasis added.)[28]

He also promised his tax cut would not get in the way of reducing the national debt, saying, "This is my approach: tax relief for everybody . . . while still reducing our national debt and funding important priorities."[29]

Well, he was wrong. And that's putting it delicately. Cynics would say Dubya knew all along he was deceiving us; that he understood you can't cut taxes, boost defense and balance the budget; that if the Reagan years taught us anything, it was that tax cuts for the rich leave a legacy of deficit and debt and drift and recession. But I'm not a cynic. I prefer to believe that our president was ignorant. Especially when the alternative is that he was purposefully deceiving us.

The Blame Game

One of the most amusing sights in Washington these days is to watch the folks who came here promising to usher in a "responsibility era" struggle and strain to pin the blame for the Bush recession on someone, anyone, other than Dubya.

The first—and obvious—choice is to blame President Clinton. Never mind that trying to blame President Clinton for Bush's failed economic policy is like blaming Hank Aaron because the stiff who replaced him couldn't hit home runs, but that's our Bush. He's never one to let the sheer stupidity of an idea keep him from embracing it. And so, in a speech in Alabama, the only president we have said: "The heady days of the 90s, the boom days of the 90s, it was like we were on a binge where there was no—the horizon was forever going up. And we binged, and now we're suffering a hangover."[30]

Now, I could point out that a man with a criminal conviction for drunk driving—who had his driver's license suspended for drunk driving, who has admitted that he drank to excess in his "misspent youth" (which continued until he was 40), who once ran over the family mailbox while drunk, who challenged his father to a fistfight while drunk—is a man in a particularly poor position to throw around words like *binge* or a *hangover*.

But I won't. That's too easy.

So, I'll just refer you to the words of Sen. Hillary Rodham Clinton, who, in a widely (and wildly) acclaimed speech to the Democratic Leadership Council, opened up a can of whup-ass on the Bush boys. "Some have called the Clinton economic record a binge," she said. "Young people able to afford college, and they call that a binge? Millions climbing out of welfare and into new jobs, and that's some kind of a binge? I'm reminded of what Abraham Lincoln said when his commanders complained about Ulysses S. Grant's binges. 'Find out,' he said, 'what kind of whiskey Grant drinks, because I want to send a barrel to each of my generals.' "[31]

Having failed to pin their fiscal mismanagement on President Clinton, the Bushies shamelessly tried to suggest that the war on terrorism has been the cause of the deficits. The war in Afghanistan had cost $17 billion as of May 2002.[32] That's $2.12 billion a month. Of course, the cost has tapered off since we've quit bombing, but let us for argument's sake assume we'll continue full bore at this pace, just to see the effect on the deficit. Even at that all-out rate, we would have to be at war for 67 years to equal just the ten-year cost of the Bush tax cut.[33]

Finally, there's the trifecta fib. In October 2001, Bush was asked by a reporter in New York if his tax cuts would "eat up the surplus." The president responded, "Well, as I said in Chicago during the campaign, when asked about should the government ever deficit spend, I said only . . . if there is a national emergency, if there is a recession, or if there's a war."[34] This has become a big line for Bush—one he uses in policy speeches, at fund-raising dinners, during press conferences. It's his way of responding to charges about vanishing surpluses and the billions spent from Social Security and Medicare Trust Funds.[35] He even likes to play it for a laugh, as he did last February while raising money for Republicans in North Carolina: "You know, I was campaigning in Chicago, and somebody asked me: 'Is there ever any time where the budget might have to go into deficit?' I said, 'Only if we were at war or had a national emergency or were in recession.' Little did I realize we'd get the trifecta!"[36]

There's only one problem with Bush's favorite line: It's not true. He made it up. There's no record of him having ever said anything of the sort during the campaign, either in Chicago or anywhere else. Not a single journalist who covered his presidential run remembers such a statement. The White House can't produce a shred of evidence to corroborate the president's claim.[37]

As *The New Republic* reported: "Not only did Bush make no exception for emergencies, but he specifically promised that even if emergencies arose, they would not force him to break his pledge. On February 27, 2001, in his first address before Congress, Bush assured that his budget would 'prepare for the unexpected, for the uncertainties of the future' by setting aside 'a contingency fund for emergencies or additional spending needs' totaling 'almost a trillion dollars.'"[38] (In case you're wondering what happened to that contingency fund—we sure could use it right about now—the answer, as you might have guessed, is that it never existed.)

When pressed to back up their boss's story, the Bushies shrug it off: Bush's Budget Director Mitch Daniels told Tim Russert, "I'm not the White House librarian."[39]

Doctor Dubya's Miracle Elixir

In Bush's defense, he does seem to have a nearly mystical devotion to cutting taxes. Of course, that's if you set aside his ardent campaign for a sales-tax increase in Arlington, Texas, the proceeds of which contributed $135 million to a brand-new stadium for Bush's baseball team. The Rangers's new stadium, with its fancy luxury boxes, was the biggest reason Bush and his cronies were able to parlay their initial investment into big cash when they sold the team. Bush's take of the tax-increase–funded scheme: almost $15 million. So, I shouldn't say Junior is irrevocably opposed to tax increases. He loved one that raised taxes on working people and put the money straight into his pocket.[40]

His own taxpayer-generated fortune aside, Bush the politician has found it handy to champion tax cuts. When he first proposed his tax cut—way back in December 1999—he did so to head off a political charge from antitax zealot Steve Forbes, one of his rivals for the Republican presidential nomination. At that time, we were still enjoying the unprecedented prosperity of the Clinton economy, so W. told his audience he was proposing "a tax cut designed to sustain our nation's prosperity."[41]

He also touted tax cuts' effect on reducing the size of government, while stimulating growth, saying, "We need to cut taxes to keep government lean, but more importantly, we need to cut taxes to continue economic growth."[42]

Later, after Bush became president and the economy softened, Bush had the answer: tax cuts. "I strongly believe," he said, "that a tax relief plan is an important part of helping our country's economy recover."[43]

You get the feeling that you just know what Bush says to people who complain to him about their neighbor's dog barking at night or burning the meatloaf or the heartbreak of psoriasis. You got it: tax cuts. That'll cure ya.

Stimulate This

Bush's tax cut for the rich passed in the summer of 2001. But by fall, things were getting worse, not better. A headline in the *Los Angeles Times* captured the grim new economic reality: JOBLESS CLAIMS HIT 450,000, A 9-YEAR HIGH.[44] You would think that new problems demand new solutions; that an economic plan developed during a boom would have to be significantly altered in a bust, but you're not George W. Bush. Oh, he changed all right. Changed his rhetoric. All of a sudden, the tax cuts that were supposed to prevent a recession were now the way to *cure* the recession. As unemployment began to spike—rising from a Clinton low of 3.9 percent to a Bush high (so far) of 5.9 percent—Dr. Dubya had just the cure for what ails us: you guessed it. "In order to stimulate the economy," he said, "Congress does not need to spend any more money; what they need to do is to cut taxes."[45]

So, just months after his massive tax cuts for the wealthy failed to stimulate the economy, George W. Bush came up with Plan B: More tax cuts for the wealthy. This time, it was for wealthy corporations instead of wealthy people. You gotta admire the guy's consistency—in the face of all evidence. George W. Bush calling for more tax cuts for the rich is like the captain of the *Titanic* calling for more icebergs.

However, that's precisely what Dubya and his Republican allies on Capitol Hill did. On October 24, 2001, the House of Representatives passed an economic stimulus measure written by GOP members of the Ways and Means Committee. The bill passed on a party line vote of 216–214, with 212 Republicans, 3 Democrats and 1 independent voting in favor.[46]

Although drafted by congressional Republicans, Bush was quick to embrace the plan. His administration issued a formal Statement of Administration Policy saying, "The administration strongly supports House passage of H.R. 3090. The administration is pleased that the House has started the process of acting on a stimulus package to help get the economy going again following the terrorist attacks of September 11th."[47]

A Quarter-Billion Dollars for Enron; Billions More for Other Corporations

The new Bush-GOP so-called stimulus package had one feature that should win an award for chutzpah: It called for a repeal of the Alternative Minimum Tax for corporations. The corporate AMT was enacted in 1986, and ensures that firms pay a minimum amount of federal income tax despite qualified deductions. Before Congress created it, 129 of the wealthiest and most successful corporations paid no federal income tax at all. Instead, they received an average tax rebate of 9.6 percent for a total of $6.4 billion.[48] So Congress passed a corporate Alternative Minimum Tax, signed into law by that notorious big-taxing liberal, Ronald Reagan.

The Bush-GOP bill would end the corporate Alternative Minimum Tax. And as if that weren't enough, it repealed the tax *retroactively*. That is, in addition to never again having to pay the tax, all the big corporations that had paid it would have it refunded—15 years' worth of back taxes . . . refunded. It did this by returning to corporations, in one big, fat check, the total amount of AMT the corporation had paid over the 15-year life of the AMT.[49]

Can you believe that? Can you really believe that Bush was ready to send the biggest corporations in America a huge check like that? Of course you can. What you wouldn't believe is if Bush had promised to rebate working people's payroll taxes for the last 15 years. Don't worry. The thought of sending you back some of your past taxes never crossed his mind.

Repealing and rebating the corporate AMT was not cheap. The cost of the House corporate AMT repeal would be $25.4 billion in the first year alone. An analysis by Citizens for Tax Justice found that 16 Fortune 500 corporations—just 16—would receive rebate checks totaling $7.4 billion, with each of those lucky 16 corporations receiving over $100 million.[50]

Capitol Hill insiders called the issue *AMT*—the initials of the Alternative Minimum Tax. But a better name would have been *ROI*—Return on Investment, because that's what the huge, avaricious corporations got: a massive return on their investments in Junior and his fellow Republicans. Bush and the GOP received $6,270,249 from the companies that would benefit the most under the House GOP's repeal of the corporate AMT.[51]

Here's who they are, what they gave and what they got.

Enron

Enron's board of directors and political action committee have given $2,052,418 to Bush and the Republicans since 1993.[52]

Under the Bush-House GOP economic stimulus plan, Enron would receive a $254 million refund; a quarter of a billion (with a B) dollars of your tax dollars, straight into the pockets of Kenny-Boy and the rest of Bush's pals at Enron. All for contributing a measly two mil over seven years (and that total, like all those in this section, includes soft money, hard money, campaign committee contributions—everything I could find).[53]

Chevron

Since 1993, members of Chevron's board of directors and Chevron's political action committee have given more than $1,154,429 to Bush and other key Republicans.[54]

Under the Bush-supported House GOP economic stimulus plan, Chevron would get a $314 million refund from tax credits it has accrued under the corporate AMT since 1986.[55]

Ford

Since 1993, the Ford Motor Company's board of directors and political action committee have given $682,698 to Bush and the Republicans.[56] Ford was the largest single corporate winner under the Bush-House GOP stimulus plan, Ford Motor Company would receive a $2.329 billion refund from the American taxpayers; a return of all the Alternative Minimum Tax Ford had paid for the previous 15 years.[57]

General Electric

Members of General Electric's board of directors and the company political action committee have given $693,792 to Bush and the Republicans since 1993.[58]

General Electric stood to receive a $671 million refund under the Bush-House GOP stimulus plan.[59]

General Motors

Members of General Motors' board of directors and the company political action committee have given $441,950 to Bush and the Republicans since 1993.[60]

Under the Bush-supported House GOP economic stimulus plan, General Motors would receive a $832 million refund from tax credits it has accrued under the corporate AMT since 1986.[61]

Kmart

Members of Kmart's board of directors and the company political action committee have given $599,262 to Bush and the Republicans since 1993.[62]

Under the Bush-supported House GOP economic stimulus plan, Kmart would have received a $102 million refund.[63]

Kroger

Members of Kroger's board of directors and the company political action committee have given $55,700 to Bush and the Republicans since 1993.[64]

Under the Bush-House GOP stimulus plan, Kroger would receive a $9 million refund.[65]

USX

Members of USX's board of directors and the company political
action committee have given $612,500 to Bush and the Republicans
since 1993.[66]

Under the Bush-House GOP stimulus plan, USX would receive a
$39 million refund.[67]

Not a bad return on investment, is it?

Actually, I'm not suggesting that those corporations gave those
contributions in order to win their huge tax breaks. Nor am I imply-
ing that there was a direct *quid pro quo* between the donations and the
tax rebates. Politics is not often that up front. Rather, the happy coincidence of the Republicans' (especially W's) affection for the moneyed interests, and the moneyed interests affection for . . . well . . .
their money.

I *will* say it was a marriage made in heaven. The Republicans had
the power and needed money for their campaigns. The corporate
special interests had money but needed power, especially on Capitol
Hill. What the god of greed has joined together, let no man put asun-
der. Praise the Lord and pass the collection plate.

Even conservative economists were aghast at this unholy matri-
mony. Bruce Bartlett, an economist who served under Presidents
Reagan and Bush and who's now with the National Center for Policy
Analysis, admitted that the Bush-GOP plan to repeal and rebate the
corporate AMT went too far. "[G]iving back the AMT credits was a
little over the top. Politically, it's untenable," Bartlett said.[68]

Bush and the bandits didn't stop there. They also proposed cutting *another* tax paid primarily by the rich: the capital gains tax, the
tax paid when you sell stocks or bonds, or polo ponies, or that spare
yacht you've outgrown. (Never mind that President Clinton had just
cut this tax four years earlier.) The Bush-GOP economic stimulus bill
called for cutting the capital gains tax from 20 percent to 18 percent.[69]

An analysis by the nonpartisan Citizens for Tax Justice found that such a reduction in the capital gains tax would benefit . . . if I have to finish this sentence, you're clearly missing the point of Bush's whole philosophy. In case you *haven't* guessed it yet, Bush's proposal would benefit wealthy taxpayers most. Over 70 percent of the tax cut would go to the top 1 percent of wage earners—folks whose annual incomes are $384,000 or more. In contrast, only 2.4 percent of the tax cut would go to the bottom 80 percent of wage earners, that is, everyone whose income is below $75,000 a year.[70]

Yes, Virginia, there is a Santa Claus.

There was only one problem with the Bush-GOP stimulus plan. The sort of niggling, picayune detail pointy-headed know-it-alls were always pointing out. Economists said it wasn't going to stimulate anything—except maybe GOP campaign donations.

According to the Center on Budget and Policy Priorities, the non-partisan Congressional Research Service (CRS) reported that "a capital gains tax cut appears the least likely of any permanent tax cut to stimulate the economy in the short run; a temporary capital gains cut is unlikely to provide any stimulus."[71]

The CRS wasn't alone. In a September meeting with the Senate Finance Committee to discuss the economic stimulus package, Federal Reserve Chairman Alan Greenspan and former Treasury Secretary Robert Rubin "advised Congress against cutting the capital gains tax, the favored approach among many Republicans on Capitol Hill."[72] Greenspan said that a capital gains tax cut would not stimulate the economy in the short run. Greenspan later reiterated his opposition to cutting the capital gains tax during an appearance before the Joint Economic Committee that October.[73]

But what do Alan Greenspan and Bob Rubin know, anyway? Do they have MBAs from Harvard, like Dubya? Nooooooo.

Economic genius that he is, Dubya proposed accelerating the already passed tax cuts, many of which were not slated to take effect for years—perhaps to mask their devastating effect on the deficit. This, too, had the virtue of rewarding those poor, oppressed millionaires. An analysis by the Citizens for Tax Justice found that accelerating the Bush income tax cuts would give most of the money to the wealthiest Americans. The top 1 percent would receive 55.3 percent of the tax cuts. The top 10 percent, those earning $108,000 or more, would receive 81.6 percent of the tax cuts.[74] In contrast, the study found that three out of four taxpayers would get "exactly zero" from the administration's proposal.[75]

Of course, the 75 percent of us who were excluded from Bush's proposed accelerated tax cut probably didn't need it. We probably would have just spent it on rent, or baby food, or clothes for the winter. However, put those billions in the hands of the rich—people who really know how to spend, and you'll see the casinos of Monte Carlo swelling, and the offshore bank accounts of the Cayman Islands filling. And if America's economic policy doesn't help those who are savvy enough to enjoy life to the fullest, what good is it?

Alan S. Blinder, a Princeton University economist and former vice chairman of the Federal Reserve, criticized Bush's plan to accelerate his income tax cuts for the rich in unusually blunt terms. "That's a terrible idea," said Blinder.[76] David Wyss, the chief economist at Standard & Poor's in New York, said that the Bush plan would not help stimulate the economy. "Rich people have this nasty habit of saving money. That's how they got rich," Wyss said.[77]

Perhaps Dr. Blinder and Dr. Wyss don't know about the Monte Carlo–Caymans effect, described above. Or perhaps—just perhaps— Dubya was using the cover of "stimulus" to do what he loves best: help the overprivileged.

Fortunately, the Democrats in the Senate—made a majority by the defection of Vermont's Jim Jeffords—were able to kill the Bush-House GOP rebate for the poor, downtrodden and dispossessed *Fortune* 500.

Repeal the Dead Billionaires' Tax!

The estate tax is the most progressive tax in America; that is, only the very wealthiest dead people pay it (or, more accurately, their heirs do). Even before the Congress cut the estate tax as part of Bush's 2001 tax cut for the rich, only 43,000 people per year paid the tax.[78] All the rest of us were exempt. This is a tax that only 1.4 percent of Americans pay; 98.6 percent of us are exempt.[79] And two-thirds of the tax is paid by the ultra-mega-hyper-uber-wealthy: the top 0.21 percent.[80]

Senate Democrats proposed exempting even more families, including virtually every single family farm and small business in

America. That wasn't good enough for Dubya. He insists on a total repeal of the billionaires' tax.[81] No traitor to his class, this trust-fund baby wants to fight for the rights of the idle rich. Apparently he's never heard the warning of Andrew Carnegie—the Bill Gates of his time—who said, a century ago, that, "The parent who leaves his son enormous wealth generally deadens the talents and energies of the son, and leads him to a less useful and less worthy life than he otherwise would."[82]

Doesn't that sound like ol' Andrew was eerily prescient? At least about the first forty years of the life of the only president we have these days. As the Citizens for Tax Justice note, "You'd think that Republicans, if anyone, would sympathize with Carnegie's point. After all, if giving a single mother $10,000 a year in welfare stifles her incentive to work, just think how much worse it must be for someone who gets a windfall of 1,000 times that much."[83]

Repealing the estate tax permanently would hand $60 billion a year to just a few thousand families. $60 billion.[84] But, the Republicans say, it's our money. Why should we be taxed on it twice—once when we earn it and once when we die?

Au contraire, mon ami. Once you're dead it ain't your money. You're dead. Not to put too fine a point on it, but when you're standin' at those pearly gates with your knees knockin', making your case to Saint Peter, the disposition of your billions is going to be the last thing on your mind. And, if you make it to Paradise, my guess is your money worries are over. And if you don't . . . well . . . you've got bigger things to worry about.

The issue here is one of personal responsibility, and rewarding work. If a maid busts her butt to earn $20,000 a year, she pays taxes on it. If an entrepreneur busts his butt, invents a new widget and makes $20 million, he pays taxes on that, too. However, if Thurston Howell IV sits on his fat ass and inherits $200 million because the old man finally croaked, why the hell should he collect it without paying a penny in taxes? Taxing work and exempting wealth is Bush's dream—and you can see why. His work ethic ain't the greatest. He seems to believe that hard work never killed anyone, but why take a chance? And yet he's fabulously wealthy—mostly because of the name and the money and the contacts he inherited. No wonder he doesn't want to tax inheritances.

The One Tax Junior Doesn't Want to Cut

There is one. So far as I can tell, only one. But there is a tax that George Walker Bush hasn't called for cutting:

The payroll tax.

This issue gives us a window into the very soul of Bushonomics. The Congressional Budget Office tells us that 80 percent of working Americans pay more in payroll taxes than they do in income taxes.[85] That's because of two things: First, Ronald Reagan raised the payroll tax on working people, and second, Bill Clinton cut the income tax for working people through his Earned Income Tax Credit. So, now, the combination of Reagan's tax increase on working folks and Clinton's tax cut for them means that four out of five working Americans pay more in the payroll tax than in income taxes.

By contrast, most of the federal income tax is paid by the rich. In fact, 80 percent of all the money Washington rakes in from income taxes comes from the wealthiest one-fifth of all Americans. By targeting the income tax—and the estate tax—for his tax cuts, Bush is playing the class warfare game his own way: cutting the taxes that hit the rich hardest, while ignoring the tax that hits 80 percent of us hardest. It's as if he chose to cut taxes on caviar instead of hamburger; champagne instead of beer; yachts instead of bass boats.

I'll say this for Junior: he can hold his head up with pride when he's at the country club. He's delivered more for the overprivileged than even the best butler ever could.

The Bottom Line

George W. Bush is rich. George W. Bush hates taxes. Especially on the rich. So if you're rich, and you hate taxes, you should love Bush.

Unless, of course, you're concerned about the nation's fiscal health, or the future of Social Security, or economic growth, or fair taxes for everyone, or any of the things that truly make for a strong, sustained economy. In that case, you're probably not a big beneficiary of the Bush tax policy.

THREE

Social Security:
Strap Granny into the Roller Coaster

"For years, politicians in both parties have dipped into the [Social Security] Trust Fund to pay for more spending. And I will stop it."—Then-Governor George W. Bush: Rancho Cucamonga, California, 4/14/00, *Washington Post* (4/15/00).

"Another priority is retirement systems of Americans. And so the budget I set up says that payroll taxes are only going to be spent on one thing, and that's Social Security."—President George W. Bush Remarks at National Newspaper Association 40th Annual Government Affairs Conference (3/22/01).

"The White House is backing away from its pledge to protect every cent of Social Security reserves in the face of a report today that the government is tapping Social Security taxes for other purposes."—*USA Today* (8/28/01).

"Contrary to campaign pledges to wall off the Social Security trust fund from other uses, Mr. Bush proposes using all the Social Security surpluses—and then borrowing from the general public beyond that—to fund the government for the next two years, and to spend well over $100 billion of Social Security funds in each of the following three years."—*Wall Street Journal* (2/5/02).

"Over the decade, Bush's budget would tap $1.8 trillion in Social Security surpluses to pay for other government programs."—Associated Press (3/6/02).

"They want the federal government controlling Social Security, like it's some kind of federal program"—Then-Governor George W. Bush, St. Charles, Missouri, 11/2/00. *Washington Post* (11/3/00).

WHEN GEORGE W. BUSH WAS RUNNING FOR PRESIDENT, HE PROMISED to allow young people to invest a portion of their Social Security in the stock market, but to do so in a way that would not reduce benefits. He also promised that he'd pass a massive tax cut, while guaranteeing that every penny from the payroll tax goes to Social Security. He joined Al Gore's call for a lockbox for Social Security revenue, swearing not to raid the Social Security Trust Fund. He told seniors at the Rancho Cucamonga Senior Center in California, "For years, politicians in both parties have dipped into the [Social Security] Trust Fund to pay for more spending. And I will stop it."[1]

While I don't like Bush, I really don't want to call him a liar. It's rude and disrespectful to call the president—even a court-appointed, unelected president—a liar. So, no, good manners will preclude me from calling Dubya a liar.

So, let's just say he fibbed.

Or, more elegantly, he was engaging in a rather daring form of mendacity.

The $1.8 Trillion Raid of the Social Security Trust Fund

In March 2001, Bush repeated his pledge that Social Security would remain in a lockbox: "Another priority is retirement systems of Americans. And so the budget I set up says that payroll taxes are only going to be spent on one thing, and that's Social Security."[2]

A year later, however, after his massive tax cut for the rich had become law, the truth emerged. On March 6, 2002, the Congressional Budget Office (CBO) released a report that said, "over the decade, Bush's budget would tap $1.8 trillion in Social Security surpluses to pay for other government programs."[3]

According to the February 5, 2002, *Wall Street Journal,* "Contrary to campaign pledges to wall off the Social Security trust fund from other uses, Mr. Bush proposes using all the Social Security surpluses—and then borrowing from the general public beyond that—to fund the government for the next two years, and to spend well over $100 billion of Social Security funds in each of the following three years."

One week later, the *Journal* uncovered "unpublished administration tables [that] show the government tapping nearly $500 billion of Social Security funds for other programs from 2008 to 2012.

Several months after the *Journal*'s report, the White House finally came clean. As *USA Today* reported, "the White House is backing away from its pledge to protect every cent of Social Security reserves in the face of a report today that the government is tapping Social Security taxes for other purposes."[4]

And that doesn't count Bush's raid on the Medicare Trust Fund. Adding the amount siphoned off from Medicare, the grand total of Bush's theft is $2 trillion over ten years.[5]

The level of cynicism on Junior's part is staggering. Al Gore, you may recall, flogged Dubya throughout the 2000 campaign over the lockbox—the pledge to safeguard all Social Security funds for Social Security alone. So, pressed by Gore, Bush promised not to spend a dime of the trust fund. Now he's spending *$1.8 trillion* from the Social Security Trust Fund, and another *$200 billion* from the Medicare Trust Fund.

Stacking the Deck on the
Social Security Privatization Commission

On May 2, 2001, President Bush signed an executive order creating a commission to recommend ways in which to increase the solvency of Social Security, which forecasters said was due to experience a financial shortfall in 2038. Usually when a president appoints such a commission it is to ensure that he hears all voices—that people who are not powerful congressmen or rich lobbyists or big-shot campaign donors can be heard as well. Often, the purpose of such presidential commissions is to tap experts in complicated areas of policy. Sometimes, it is to provide a prestigious forum for various opinions.

Not for our man Dubya. Without a trace of shame, he stacked the deck of the Social Security Commission with people who already held his radical view that Social Security should be at least partially privatized.

I'll say this for Bush: He wasn't cute about it. He had his spokesman, Ari Fleischer, make it clear to the press that the fix was in. "The commission that the president will announce will, of course, be comprised of people who share the president's view that personal retirement accounts are the way to save Social Security."[6]

Quick translation: *personal retirement accounts* is Bushspeak for privatizing Social Security. There's nothing stopping you from having a personal retirement account today. In fact, every American with a 401(k) or an IRA or even a savings account can call it a "personal retirement account." However, that's not the goal for the Bushies. Privatizing Social Security is. And that's where the commission was supposed to come in handy.

Bush appointed 16 members—distinguished Americans all—and named then-74-year-old retired Democratic Senator Daniel Patrick Moynihan and AOL–Time-Warner executive Richard Parsons as its co-chairs.

There's an old saying that, if two people agree on everything, one of them's not necessary. Well, the Bush Social Security Commission had 16 people who agreed on the most important thing—that we should turn part of Social Security over to the tender mercies of the stock market. According to the *New York Times,* potential members to the commission "had been screened to ensure that its members would overwhelmingly or perhaps unanimously endorse private accounts," and, according to the *Los Angeles Times,* members "assured the White House that they share Bush's ideas for changing the system, foremost of which is allowing its partial privatization."[7]

Hardly a reflection of American popular opinion. Nor was it reflective of experts on the issue. Terry Moran of ABC News described the strategy accurately: "The president likes to portray himself as above politics, but the strategy that he revealed today to push his Social Security privatization plan is about as slick and as hardball as it gets."[8]

Martha A. McSteen, president of the National Committee to Preserve Social Security and Medicare, blasted the stacked deck, saying, "If the commission is to truly serve the public interest, it must go beyond its narrow mandate and consider a number of the alternative proposals for improving the financial health of the Social Security program without relying on risky privatization schemes. President Bush promised to change the partisan tone of politics in Washington, but neither the composition nor the mandate of the commission reflect a serious attempt to build consensus on a middle of the road solution."[9]

The most respected organization on retirement issues, the AARP, weighed in to protest the obvious bias of the commission. Horace Deets, executive director of AARP, said the Bush commission "appears to lack a balance of viewpoints, which suggests its recommendations will not develop in a way that will lead to the broad support needed for action."[10]

None of this deterred Bush, however. The supporters of Social Security were merely stating the obvious: The Bush Social Security plan was not on the level.

News Flash: Bush-Appointed Commission Endorses Bush Plan

Part of the genius of George W. Bush is his obviousness. Like when he wanted to convince the reform-minded McCain voters in the Republican primaries that he was a reformer, too—but a reformer with results. So, he gave a speech in which he proclaimed himself "a reformer with results" and stood in front of a giant backdrop with the phrase (have you guessed it?) *Reformer with Results* emblazoned about a thousand times. Subtle, eh?

About as subtle as the Bush Social Security Commission. Having appointed only people who had sworn fealty to his idea of partially privatizing Social Security, Bush turned them loose to pursue the facts without fear or favor. And can you imagine? The commission came back—and this is going to be hard for you to believe—with an endorsement of Bush's plan to partially privatize Social Security!

I am not making this up.

The problem for Bush was that the commission got specific. Way more specific than Bush had ever dared to be. The commission's specifics are pretty scary:

Cutting Social Security Benefits

In November 2001, the President's Social Security Commission released an outline of three plans to privatize Social Security. All three of the commission's plans reduce your guaranteed Social Security benefits if you participate in the partial privatization (and even in some cases if you don't, which we will get to in a moment).

So, if you're smart (and lucky) and you invest in a winner, part of your reward is a reduction in your guaranteed Social Security benefit. The Bush proposals are thus more like investing in the stock market on margin—you borrow the money you're going to invest in Wall Street from the guaranteed benefits you would have from the Social Security Trust Fund. And, you have to pay it back regardless of how well your portfolio performs. So, if your stocks go up, you still have to pay back the amount you initially diverted from the trust fund. But if they go down, you not only lose the gain you'd been counting on, you *still* have to pay back the initial amount you invested. And you pay it back in the form of reduced Social Security benefits.[11]

I don't remember Monty Hall trying that on *Let's Make a Deal*. But Bush's program is not *Let's Make a Deal*. It's *Let's Cut Social Security to Pay for Tax Cuts for the Rich.*

Here's another way in which Bush wants to cut your guaranteed Social Security benefits: Currently, Social Security benefits are indexed to growth in wages, but one of the commission's plans proposes indexing benefits to inflation, a move that could cut benefits by close to 50 percent. Fifty percent. Cut in half! (Some of these important points I'm going to repeat two or three times on the off chance that Bush himself reads this book. Those of you who didn't go to Andover and Yale and Harvard like Junior will probably get it the first time.) So, just by changing the indexing, they cheat you out of half of what you'd get under the current system.

According to the *Wall Street Journal*, the plan "would gradually trim initial benefits for succeeding generations of new retirees."[12]

The cuts even hit you if you choose *not* to partially privatize your Social Security. That's right—even if you *opt out* of privatization, your benefits still get cut. For instance, under one commission proposal, here's what happens to a worker who is 35 years old today, chooses not to invest in a personal account, and retires at age 65 in 2032: his guaranteed benefits would be 17 percent less than what he could expect under the current formula. Worse, those born in 2001 and retiring in 2066 would see their guaranteed benefits reduced 41 percent.[13]

So, you've got a choice: eat dirt or drink mud. Either you climb aboard the Enron express and put your Social Security in the crapshoot of the stock market, or you get a deep cut in your Social Security benefits. Tucker Carlson told me an amazing story of a similar kind of decision. A fraternity hazed its pledges by making them stand naked and blindfolded. Then, they placed a brick in the pledge's hand, tied one end of a string to the brick and the other end to his . . . well . . . to a very sensitive part of his body. Then they put his pledge pin in the other hand and said, "Drop the one that's less important to you."

Now, the sadistic frat rats had quietly cut the string while the boy was blindfolded, so no one got hurt, but Tucker tells me there actually were boys who dropped the brick, such was their allegiance to the frat.[14] I never did join a frat. Dubya, on the other hand, was president of the Deke house at Yale. So, maybe he's just more comfortable than I am with painful decisions, 'cause he's sure trying to force one on you regarding Social Security.

Raising the Retirement Age

In 1999, during the presidential campaign, Bush told NBC's Tim Russert on *Meet the Press* that raising the retirement age "may be an option for the boomer generation."[15] As the law stands today, the retirement age is gradually due to go up from 65 to 67. So, when Bush says he might raise it even higher, you're looking at working even longer to receive the same benefit.

Bush's commission followed his lead, proposing changes in the benefit formula that would force workers to remain in the workforce longer to earn the same benefit. The proposal would reduce benefits for those who stop working at the normal retirement age or any other specific age—forcing workers to retire later to preserve their benefit levels.[16]

Now, working past age 67 is probably not the worst thing in the world if, like me, you're a cable-television blowhard and a writer. My mouth and my fingers and my smart-ass attitude will probably be just as effective at age 69 as they are today. But what about people who work for a living? I mean *really* work. Bush is telling a waitress who's breaking her back carrying trays that she's got to keep slinging hash; utility workers they've got to keep digging ditches or climbing telephone poles; factory workers they've got to work more years in hot, sweaty, difficult jobs. And how about coal miners? Firefighters? Cops?

I love the idea of a guy who's coasted on his family's wealth and connections all his life—who takes monthlong vacations, and leaves the office for a daily workout and a nap—telling working people they've got to stay on the job for years and years just to get the same retirement they thought they were getting all along.

Your Benefits Get Cut, But It *Still* Costs $1 Trillion More

How can that be? Here's how: The money ain't there. Remember the surplus? It's gone. (See the chapter on taxes and the deficit.) Turns out that when you squander $5.3 trillion of the American people's surplus you don't have much money left over for lesser priorities, like keeping Aunt Gladys from having to eat Alpo.

Okay, so the money's gone, but we still haven't explained why we need more money to give you fewer guaranteed Social Security benefits. Here's why: Economists call it a *transition cost.* The money in the box marked *FICA* (which stands for Federal Insurance Contributions Act) is really your Social Security tax. Now, I don't want to shock you, but the Social Security Administration doesn't put that money in a shoebox with your name on it, leave it there, then gift wrap it and mail it back to you for your sixty-fifth birthday. Instead, they put that money to work. Much of it goes to fund current beneficiaries. It's an intergenerational transfer payment. You parents' Social Security taxes supported your grandparents. And, now, you're supporting your parents.

But, under Bush's plan, your money won't go to support Aunt Gladys—at least, not all of it. Some of it will go to Wall Street, where it may be invested in honest, well-run companies, or perhaps placed in the grimy paws of someone like Bush's buddy Ken Lay. At the same time, Bush is promising current retirees that their benefits won't be cut.

If you put a splitter on your garden hose so you can wash the car while you're also watering the lawn, you wind up with only half as much water for each task. This is fine if you've got plenty of water coming in. What happens if suddenly your water pressure drops?

Bush's tax cut is the drop in the water pressure. With the stroke of a pen, he diverted more than $1.7 trillion away from Social Security or other national priorities, and into the pockets of some of the wealthiest people in the world.

By promising younger people that they can shift some of the taxes they pay into Social Security toward Wall Street investments, while simultaneously promising current retirees that they'll keep getting the same benefits, Bush is promising the same pot of money to two different groups.

And it's quite a pot of money. According to *Business Week*, Bush's plan "will create an even greater [Social Security] shortfall. For example, diverting two percent of payroll tax into private accounts would leave the Social Security system an additional $1 trillion short over 10 years."[17]

And $1 trillion may just be the start of the mess. Over a 20-year period, the transition costs grow to $3 trillion.[18]

That's one whale of a transition cost. It's a fiscal Moby Dick.

If you were on Wall Street and tried counting the same funds in two different places at the same time, you'd be WorldCom. If you did the same thing in the White House, you'd be George W. Bush.

Back to Deficits

The Bush Social Security plan would do for FDR's masterpiece what the Bush tax plan did for Clinton's federal budget surplus: plunge it into deficit. Did you really expect more from a guy who, in a fit of pique, attacked Al Gore and Joe Lieberman's plan to save Social Security from privatization, saying, "They want the federal government controlling Social Security, like it's some kind of federal program."[19]

According to a *Boston Globe* editorial, "Under privatization, the [Social Security] system would quickly accumulate huge deficits as part of the money that now pays benefits is diverted into younger people's individual accounts. The commission needs to estimate how big this cost would be and how it would be paid for in light of Bush's refusal to countenance a tax increase. And the commission should not count on budget surpluses to defray the cost; they might be eaten up by Bush's tax cuts."[20]

This means that, under Bush's plan, with no general revenue to pay the transition cost, he'll be forced to tap the Social Security Trust Fund. Right now that trust fund is flush, since the money you pay in

Social Security taxes (plus the interest those funds accrue) exceeds the amount we need to pay for Aunt Gladys and other current beneficiaries by $160 billion. Bush's plan would deplete the entire trust fund in 2024. (If we do nothing, nothing at all, to "save" Social Security, we won't exhaust the trust fund until 2038.)[21]

What If the Market Goes Down?

Every American with a 401(k)—or even a television—has seen the disastrous drop in the stock market recently. Fortunes have been lost, retirements have been postponed, college savings plans have been dealt a severe setback, but Social Security hasn't been damaged a bit. Even the people who lost their entire 401(k) still have the rock-solid, unbreakable, unshakable guarantee of Social Security.

What if the Bush plan to privatize Social Security had been the law? According to a study by the Center for Economic and Policy Research, as of June 30, 2002 (*before* the worst drops of July 2002), workers would have lost $31 billion had Bush's plan to allow individuals to invest 2 percentage points of payroll taxes in private accounts been in place since 1998. Allowing individuals to invest 5 percentage points would have led to losses of more than $78 billion if the policy had been in place since 1998.[22]

If you were unfortunate enough to work for Bush's buddy Kenny-Boy Lay at Enron, things would have been even worse. In addition to losing your job, your pension and your 401(k)—not to mention any stock options—you also would have lost as much as $279 a month in Social Security when you retired.[23]

And the Winner Is . . . Bush's Big-Money Buddies

Despite all this bad news, Junior, God love him, is unfazed. Even after the stock market had lost $7 trillion in two years, even after the NASDAQ had fallen by 75 percent, even after the corporate rip-offs and accounting scams, Dubya once more proclaimed his support for partial privatization of Social Security.[24]

As the inimitable and brilliant Paul Krugman noted in his *New York Times* column, millions of Americans no longer have corporate pensions that guarantee a benefit. They have, instead, what are called *defined contribution* plans in which their employer contributes X dollars (often in company stock) and the employee is left to ride it up or down. The rise of defined contribution plans makes the guarantee of Social Security more important than ever.

But not to Bush. Why? Why this pseudoreligious commitment to privatizing Social Security, despite the costs, despite the risks, despite the prospect of leaving Americans impoverished in their retirement? Krugman suggests that one reason may be that privatizing Social Security would pour tens of billions of dollars into the hands of Wall Street money managers—folks who make a commission whether you make money or not. The Center on Budget and Policy Priorities estimated that, if two percentage points of the Social Security tax were channeled to personal accounts in 2002, Wall Street firms could see $86 billion in new investment capital.[25]

Professor Krugman (he teaches economics at Princeton, as well as writing for the *Times*) notes that Bush had a very cozy relationship as governor of Texas with the money managers who handled state assets (all of which was faithfully reported in *Is Our Children Learning?*), and quotes the veteran political reporter R. G. Ratcliffe of the *Houston Chronicle*, who's been covering Bush for years. Back in 1998 Ratcliffe wrote that in Bush's dealings, "a pattern emerges: When a Bush is in power, Bush's business associates benefit."

The Bottom Line

Bush's plan to partially privatize Social Security is a threat to the most successful government social program in American history. And it is being pushed by an administration that is hostile to FDR's masterpiece. According to the *Financial Times*, Bush Treasury Secretary Paul O'Neill raised the possibility of doing away with Social Security for seniors entirely: "O'Neill questioned the guarantees the government provides for full public subsidy of senior citizens' healthcare and retirement programs. 'Able-bodied adults who have the ability to earn income have an obligation not to pass part of their own responsibility on to a broader population,' he said."[26]

At least O'Neill has the candor and the courage to put his cards on the table. Bush, however, is far too cagey for that. Dubya was certainly not the businessman O'Neill (the former CEO of Alcoa) was, but he's a far, far better fibber.

Right-wing critics call Social Security a Ponzi scheme or a shell game, but they never liked Social Security anyway—precisely for its intergenerational appeal. They believe we're all in this alone. Liberals know we're all in this together and actually feel good that their hard work is helping the greatest generation in its golden years. The tough part comes when the baby boomers enter their geriatric phase (Mick Jagger is, after all, 59 years old.)

Many of the cut-Social-Security crowd are good-hearted people who are panicked at the thought that there won't be enough workers to support them in their retirement. They're wrong. The standard analysis makes no adjustment, for example, for changing immigration patterns. What has immigration got to do with Social Security? Lots. Projections are that one day we'll have only two workers for each baby boomer retiree—unless more workers come here. And come here they will. At every other critical juncture in American history, when there was a job that was too dirty or dangerous or difficult for the native-born Americans, we turned to immigrants. That's how my people got here, and I suspect that's how yours did as well.

Even without considering immigration, the Clinton years saw a substantial increase in the projected solvency of the system, simply because the strong economy was generating so much more tax revenue than had been anticipated.

If the economy stays weak, and even if Bush's plan is blocked by congressional Democrats, Social Security may still need an infusion of cash somewhere in the middle of the twenty-first century. That's where Bush's tax cut does so much damage, and that's why repealing the portion of the Bush tax cut that hasn't yet taken effect could be so helpful. The entire shortfall in Social Security over seventy-five years is $3.7 trillion.[27] As the big-shot economists say, "That's a lot o' moolah." But get this: Over that same period of time the Bush tax cuts will cost us more than *twice* that much.

If you want to save Social Security without cutting benefits, without raising payroll taxes, without plunging Social Security into deficits and without gambling Granny's retirement on Kenny-Boy Lay's latest Wall Street scheme, there's really only one option: repeal the as-yet-unrealized portions of the Bush tax cut.

Social Security gets saved. Granny gets her benefits. Nobody gets hurt. And here's the beauty part: The only way to repeal the future Bush tax cuts is to replace Bush with a president who will actually put Social Security first.

FOUR

(Dis)Investing in People

"You teach a child to read, and he or her will be able to pass a literacy test."—George W. Bush, Townsend, Tenn., 2/21/01.[1]

"I want to thank the dozens of welfare to work stories, the actual examples of people who made the firm and solemn commitment to work hard to embetter themselves."—George W. Bush, 4/18/02.[2]

"The public education system . . . is where children from all over America learn to be responsible citizens, and learn to have the skills necessary to take advantage of our fantastic opportunistic society."—George W. Bush, Santa Clara, Calif., 4/30/02.[3]

"If a person doesn't have the capacity that we all want that person to have, I suspect hope is in the far distant future, if at all."—George W. Bush, Remarks to the Hispanic Scholarship Fund Institute, Washington, D.C., 6/30/01.[4]

"We must have the attitude that every child in America— regardless of where they're raised or how they're born—can learn."—George W. Bush, Speech in New Britain, Conn., 4/18/01.[5]

"And so, in my State of the—my State of the Union—or state— my speech to the nation, whatever you want to call it, speech to the nation—I asked Americans to give 4,000 years—4,000 hours over the next—the rest of your life—of service to America. That's what I asked—4,000 hours."—George W. Bush, Bridgeport, Conn., 4/9/02.[6]

"I believe the results of focusing our attention and energy on teaching children to read and having an education system that's responsive to the child and to the parents, as opposed to mired in a system that refuses to change, will make America what we want it to be—a literate country and a hopefuller country."—George W. Bush, Washington, D.C., 1/11/01.[7]

"Of all states that understands local control of schools, Iowa is such a state."—George W. Bush, Council Bluffs, Iowa, 2/28/01.[8]

ONE OF THE REASONS THE CLINTON ECONOMIC MIRACLE WAS SO SUCcessful was because it was built on a solid foundation. Rather than single-shot quick fixes, the Clintonians focused on three long-term strategies for growth: fiscal discipline, creating jobs through expanding trade, and investing in ideas and initiatives that make us smarter, safer and stronger.

Each of the legs of this stool is important. Let's examine the third.

When it comes to investing in people, President Bush often talks a good game. He even stole the trademarked slogan of the liberal Children's Defense Fund: Leave No Child Behind. But, as in so many other areas, his record doesn't match his rhetoric. And as Marian Wright Edelman of the aforementioned Children's Defense Fund has pointed out, "Children can't eat promises." Yet it looks like children—and the rest of us—will continue to get little more than promises from Dubya, because he went and squandered America's surplus on tax breaks for the megarich.

Let's look at the record.

Why Fund Education When Ignorance
Has Served Dubya So Well?

When George W. Bush was in the first years of his first term as governor of Texas, he had education proposals that even I could support.

He allowed the Democrats who ran the Texas legislature to craft a tax plan that would have, among other things, created a new tax paid by prosperous Texans with the revenue going to the poorer school districts of Texas. The proposal would have greatly increased the state's contribution to education funding, and gone a long way toward addressing the tragic inequities between rich and poor school districts, but his own party killed the reform, and Bush left Texas not having made an appreciable dent in equalizing funding.

And funding is what it's all about. I love it when conservatives say education can't be solved by throwing money at it. But, apparently, defense can. The United States leads the world in military spending, and Bush's request for the Pentagon's budget is more than six times larger than the total spending of country number two, Russia. In fact, we spend more than 26 times more than Iraq, Iran, Cuba, Libya, North Korea, Sudan and Syria—the nations most frequently mentioned as our adversaries—combined. And, even if you take the seven countries I just listed and throw in the combined defense budgets of Russia and China for good measure, we spend 300 percent more than they do.[9]

Don't get me wrong. I'm glad we have the strongest defense in world history, and I support large defense budgets. I'm not even going to complain that we spend more on defense than the combined spending of the countries number two through twenty-five.[10] I'm just saying that I don't want to hear my conservative friends tell me we don't have to spend more money on education because "more money is not the answer."

It *is* about funding. Just as we know that tough talk can't defeat our enemies abroad, so we ought to have learned by now that sweet speeches and phony photo ops can't defeat ignorance and poverty either.

Education Funding: Leaving Lots of Children Behind

If you want a graphic illustration of how Bush's promises don't match his performance, look no further than the experience of Senator Edward M. Kennedy. Senator Kennedy has worked with nine presidents, and he was impressed with Bush's promises on education. So, he decided to risk his prestige and work with President Bush to pass a sweeping education bill, called the No Child Left Behind Act. Bush signed it with much fanfare, and joshed about how the folks at the coffee shop in Crawford, Texas might find it hard to believe what a nice guy Teddy Kennedy was. And he flat out gave his word he'd increase education funding as the bill calls for: "The new role of the federal government," he proclaimed, "is to set high standards, provide resources, hold people accountable, and liberate school districts to meet the standards. . . . *We're going to spend more on our schools, and we're going to spend it more wisely,*" Bush said. (Emphasis added.) [11]

But, no sooner was the president's signature on the bill than he started to backtrack on his promises. The folks back at the coffee shop in Crawford would call that *crawfishing*—after the way the small crustacean skitters backward. And they wouldn't mean it as a compliment. An analysis of the Bush education budget by the House Committee on Education and the Workforce concluded: "Just one month ago, Congress and the president enacted the most important education reform legislation in 30 years. This bipartisan law is based on the principle that, with adequate resources, real reform is possible. But rather than building on this progress, *the president's budget cuts initiatives in the No Child Left Behind Act by a net total of $90 million.*" (Emphasis added.) [12]

Now, Senator Kennedy has been in politics for decades. He's no babe in the woods. He was, nonetheless, stunned by Bush's duplicity. He called the Bush education budget, "a severe blow to our nation's schools. Just four weeks after the president signed the education bill into law, the administration's budget cuts funding for it." [13]

It's a pattern with Bush. His Deputy Secretary of Education proclaimed that, "President Bush has proposed a generous budget for education in 2003." [14] In reality, President Bush proposed the smallest increase in education funding in seven years, according to the Congressional Budget Office. Despite the growing education needs of our country, as the children of the baby boomers crowd our classrooms to the breaking point, Bush only requested a 2.8 percent increase in funding for the Department of Education—barely enough to maintain purchasing power at the 2002 level. [15]

Architects like to say that "God is in the details." Lawmakers know that the devil's in the details. So let's look at the details of

Bush's education budget. Then you can decide if he's an angel . . . or something else.

Begin at the Beginning: Early Childhood Education Cut

President Bush has proposed cutting Even Start by 20 percent. Even Start is a terrific program that focuses on the educational needs of low-income families with young children. It offers tutoring to preschoolers, and literacy and job training for their parents.[16] It's exactly the kind of program that can give folks on the bottom rung of the economic ladder a leg up to the next rung. In other words, it's exactly the kind of program Bush would cut.

Short-Changing Elementary and Secondary Education

George W. Bush professes to love teachers. And, by all accounts, the teacher he married is terrific. I just wish he'd spread the love around a little more. He declared to the nation that, "We must upgrade our teacher colleges and teacher training and launch a major recruitment drive with a great goal for America: a quality teacher in every classroom." [17] Yet his budget included no new proposals for teacher recruitment, and freezes the Teacher Quality initiative. The Teacher Quality initiative helps states and school districts reduce class sizes and do a better job of recruiting and training teachers. The need for this program has not been frozen. Inflation has not been frozen. And school enrollment, far from being frozen, is growing. So, what Bush calls a *freeze* actually operates as a cut. And an unkind cut at that.[18]

Bush also proposed freezing the 21st Century Community Learning Centers program, a program that provides safe, healthy places for over 2 million children to learn after school. The Bush budget freezes this popular initiative for the second year in a row—despite the promise to boost it in the No Child Left Behind Act.[19]

Speaking of freezing, an awful lot of our kids are shivering in their classrooms in the winter. More than 15 million American children go to school and try to learn in facilities that have substandard heating, ventilation, plumbing and roofing systems. Our schools are, on average, 42 years old; nearly 25,000 public schools, almost one-third of all public school buildings, are in a serious state of disrepair. The backlog of school repairs is estimated at $127 billion. And yet, last year, inexplicably, President Bush fought for the *repeal* of a new federal initiative to modernize America's schools and provide safe, modern places to learn for all children.[20]

Perhaps, as a child of privilege who went to one of the most expensive elite private academies (Phillips Andover), Dubya just doesn't understand how much harder it is for a child to learn when she's cold, or cramped or crowded. But, surely, given his self-confessed "youthful indiscretions," Bush should understand the importance of the Safe and Drug-Free Schools Act. Nope. This successful program, a comprehensive strategy to build safe schools by reducing drugs and violence, was cut by $103 million, or 14 percent, in the Bush budget.[21]

Nor was Bush any more receptive to the special needs of special education students. One of the great success stories of the last quarter-century has been special education. On December 2, 1975, the Education for All Handicapped Act was signed into law by President Gerald Ford. Since then, the bill has been renamed the Individuals with Disabilities Education Act, or IDEA, and it has helped a generation of children with special needs enter the mainstream of American life. However, the federal government never fully funded IDEA. As a candidate, George W. Bush attacked the lack of funding, saying, "IDEA is a good idea. But it's an unfunded mandate. My goal is to work with Congress to get IDEA fully funded. Properly funded, the program will help children with disabilities receive a better education and help local school districts provide a better education."[22] Now, if you'd read that interview during the campaign, you would have thought that Bush wanted to fully fund IDEA, given that he said so and all. But you would be wrong.

To fully fund IDEA, the federal government would need to contribute 40 percent of the cost of educating each special ed student. (The rest would come from state and local governments.) But President Bush's budget funded less than half the percentage contribution authorized under IDEA—just 17 percent.[23] The Senate, God bless 'em, voted to correct Bush's error. Led by Democratic Senator Tom Harkin of Iowa—one of the great champions of disabled Americans—and Republican Senator Chuck Hagel of Nebraska, the Senate voted to fully fund the federal share of special education as required under the Individuals with Disabilities Education Act. The Harkin-Hagel amendment increased Bush's proposed funding level by a built-in increase of

$2.5 billion a year until 2007, at which point special ed would be fully funded—and Bush's campaign promise kept.[24]

You might imagine Bush would be relieved that the Senate had corrected his mistake. And you'd be wrong again. Far from being grateful to the Senate for making good on one of his campaign promises, the Bush administration called the Harkin-Hagel amendment to fully fund special ed "costly and unwarranted."[25]

Costly and unwarranted. Educating specially challenged kids is costly and unwarranted. If that doesn't burn you up, you've got asbestos in your blood.

Next to special ed students, the kids who are the most deserving of federal aid are the poorest of the poor. In his well-received speeches, President Bush seems to agree. He said, "We have a special obligation to disadvantaged children to close the achievement gap in our nation."[26] Title I is the primary funding device for underprivileged children's education. Under the Bush budget, the number of poor children left behind by Title I is projected to grow by 250,000.[27] In his budget, President Bush did propose a small increase in Title I, but sought to redistribute the money in such a way that seven states—Delaware, Iowa, Maine, Mississippi, New Hampshire, Ohio and Utah—would see their Title I funding reduced. What's worse, 4,298 school districts—29 percent of all the school districts in America—would have lost their Title I funding altogether.[28]

On May 3, 2001, every Democratic senator voted to fully fund Title I, making sure it reaches every eligible student—a $132 billion increase in funding for the program over 10 years. The amendment would increase Title I funding in next year by $6.4 billion, bringing the total to $15 billion—almost $6 billion more than Bush had proposed.[29]

According to *Congressional Quarterly,* "White House officials and some Senate Republicans had resisted efforts by Democrats to increase Title I spending enough to reach all eligible schoolchildren. The program reaches 33 percent of those students at its current level of funding."[30]

In an age when more parents are working, after school programs are more important than ever. One of the most successful after school programs, the 21st Century Community Learning Centers, provides safe and healthy places for over 2 million children to learn after school and before their parents get home from work. The No Child Left Behind Act that Bush signed called for $1.5 billion in funding for these after school programs. Our president's budget sought to freeze it instead at $1 billion.[31]

And then, who can ever forget when Dubya's daddy, Poppy, was reported to have been stunned by the technological wizardry of the grocery-store scanner. In truth, I think it was a bad rap but, regardless, you'd think the experience would have sealed Bush's commitment to education technology. Wrong again. Bush's budget sought to cut $122 million from federal technology education programs. He proposed eliminating programs including Preparing Tomorrow's Teachers to Use Technology, Star Schools and Community Technology Centers. He wanted to freeze other technology education initiatives, despite research that shows that applying technology can increase students' test scores.[32]

Even if they don't have technology, children learn better in smaller classrooms, especially in the early years. Dubya doesn't seem to get this. As governor, he effectively called for eliminating Texas's limit on class size. Said it was an infringement on local control.[33] He didn't do any better as president. President Bush's budget proposed eliminating the Class Size Reduction program, and block-granting it with five other education programs, putting funds for smaller classes at risk. Under the Class Size Reduction program, initiated by President Clinton and fought for by Democrats in Congress, $1.6 billion has been authorized to hire 37,000 additional teachers to reduce class size for 1.9 million students. By throwing the class size initiative into the same pot with five other programs, then letting states untangle the mess, Bush put at risk one of the most widely agreed upon education reforms.[34]

The president's budget for elementary and secondary education proposed cutting 56 education programs totaling $1.7 billion. Programs that fell under his ax include Civic Education, Dropout Prevention, the National Writing Project and Preparing Tomorrow's Teachers to Use Technology. The Fund for the Improvement of Education—which supports small schools, arts education, community technology centers, and gifted and talented education—was to be cut by 90 percent.[35]

Higher Education: Slamming Shut the Doors of College

Few federal programs have done more good for more deserving Americans than the Pell Grant program. About 23 percent of all students at four-year colleges—and 45 percent of African-American and Hispanic students—depend on Pell Grants.[36] The grants are named for the legendary (now retired) Senator Claiborne Pell, a Rhode Island patrician who believed deeply in extending opportunity to people who were not born with a trust fund. Bush, too, is a patrician. He, too, was born with a trust fund. But he somehow lacks Senator Pell's commitment to doing more for those who were born with less.

In 1976, a Pell Grant covered 84 percent of the cost of attending a public university. Today, it only covers 40 percent. In order for a Pell Grant to be worth today what it was worth in 1976, it would have to be $7,000.[37] As a presidential candidate, George W. Bush pledged to provide $5,100 Pell Grants to low-income college freshmen. As president, his budget proposed a maximum Pell Grant of just $3,850—slightly more than half of what such a grant was worth in the '70s. And Dubya's 2003 budget freezes the maximum Pell Grant at this year's $4,000 level.[38]

In February 2002, Bush was getting heat for a $1.3 billion dollar shortfall in the Pell Grant program—the funding level that the president signed into law only months ago. So, he asked Congress to close the gap—by cutting promised funding to literacy, computer, and teacher-training programs, as well as construction projects.[39]

Maybe he was hoping if he cut literacy funding those affected would be unable to read about it.

The Bush budget also proposed freezing funding for the Leveraging Educational Assistance Partnerships (LEAP). The LEAP program encourages states to establish need-based grant programs by requiring them to match federal funding dollar for dollar. By leveraging state dollars, LEAP provided $171 million to low-income students last year. Bush's 2003 budget proposed eliminating the $67 million LEAP program, potentially affecting 1.2 million recipients.[40] He also proposed freezing funding for the Federal Perkins Loan—a low-interest (5 percent) loan for both undergraduate and graduate students with exceptional financial need.[41]

Perhaps the Bushies' biggest public mistake on higher education funding issues was when, in April 2002, the White House proposed preventing college students and graduates from consolidating their education loans at federally subsidized, fixed interest rates. The GOP plan would have allowed the consolidated loans to be offered only at variable rates, making the loans less appealing and more expensive.[42] The Bush plan would effectively raise interest rates for the 700,000 student borrowers who consolidate or refinance their federal student loans each year. A typical borrower with $16,928 in federal student loan debt would be charged $2,800 more over the total loan period if he or she were unable to consolidate loans at the 4 percent fixed rate. Additionally, the typical Pell Grant borrower with $18,928 in federal loan debt would be charged about $3,100 more.[43] Fortunately, Congressional Democrats stopped that Bush plan cold.

In all, the Bush budget called for helping 375,800 *fewer* low-income students pay for college. Bush asked Congress to cut 65,000 students from the College Work Study Program, 48,000 from Perkins Loans, 72,000 from Leveraging Educational Assistance Partnerships and 55,000 from TRIO, a program that assists low-income, disabled and first-generation college students.[44]

Some of these proposed cuts were averted by the Democrats, but that's not the point. The point is that George W. Bush talks a good game on education, but he'd rather spend your money on tax cuts for his wealthy friends than education for your kids.

Other Cuts

The Bush budget for fiscal year 2003 proposed cutting the Labor Department's budget by $2.9 billion, a 4.8 percent cut. The budget cuts would come from the agencies that enforce job-safety standards, minimum-wage requirements and job-training programs, including several programs to help laid-off workers get new jobs[45]. Here's where Bush's tax cut and his social-policy agenda work hand-in-glove. The Bush deficit means something has to be cut to pay for the tax cuts for his wealthy contributors. So why not cut the government programs his wealthy contributors hate the most? The ones that protect working men and women.

Cruelly, given that the Bush recession has cost 1.8 million Americans their jobs, our president called for eliminating eight different job-training programs within the Labor Department, and 12 other job-training programs run by other departments.[46] Similarly, his budget called for cutting the Youth Opportunity Grants Program from $225 million to $45 million. This program helps young people in high-poverty areas and, according to the AFL-CIO and the U.S. Conference of Mayors, was cost effective and "has yielded impressive results." Bush's budget would fund the first round of grants announced for their full five years, but would not fund any additional rounds of grants. Even Bush's Labor Secretary, Elaine Chao, has boasted of these programs, saying, "These grants are early intervention funds to build our twenty-first century workforce. For our country to have the prepared workforce it needs, we can't afford to let at-risk youths slip through our fingers."[47]

You're right, Madam Secretary. Why do you suppose your boss wasn't listening when you were giving that speech? Maybe he was too busy trying to cut all these other job-training programs:

- **The H-1B training program.** It's named after a provision in the law that allows foreign workers to come to America if their skills are in short supply in this country. This immigration policy was especially useful for high-tech firms that couldn't find enough qualified people here. Rather than just rely on immigration, Congress created the H-1B job-training program. "The goal of the training grants," says the Department of Labor, "is to prepare Americans for [the] same high skill jobs, reducing the dependence on foreign labor."[48] Bush's budget eliminates all funding for this worthwhile program.

- **The dislocated worker programs under the Workforce Investment Act.** Bush proposed cutting it by $166 million—or 11 percent.[49]

- **Youth job-training programs under the Workforce Investment Act.** Bush proposed cutting them by $127 million. The Youth Activities funding under the Department of Labor went to programs and activities designed to help low-income youths find academic and employment success.[50]

Health and Safety Cut to Dangerous Levels

The good folks at the Occupational Safety and Health Administration have an important job to do: making sure you don't bust your ass (literally) while you're busting your ass at work (figuratively). I don't know how to tell you this, but your ass ain't as important to Bush as it is to you. He called for cutting $8.9 million from OSHA, and for eliminating 83 positions from its staff. Bush's budget cut $1.3 million from OSHA's Safety and Health Standards program and $700,000 from federal enforcement activities. It also turned an $11.2 million grant program for worker training into a $4 million grant program geared toward employers.[51]

Finally—and unbelievably—Bush's budget calls for cutting $3.6 million—6 percent—and 46 positions from the Mine Safety and Health Administration.[52] All of us who remember the heroic rescue of the courageous Pennsylvania coal miners who were trapped underground for days have caught a glimpse of the dangers mineworkers face. And many of us remember Bush rushing to a photo op with the rescued miners. Mining is dangerous work. Forty-two coal miners died in 2001, thirteen of them in a single blast in Alabama. Yet Dubya has turned his back on the miners who entrusted him with their votes. Those coal miners' votes allowed Bush to carry West Virginia, which allowed him to claim the White House. (If Al Gore had won West Virginia, it wouldn't have mattered who won Florida; Gore would be in the White House, and mine safety would not have been cut.)

The Kiss of Death

For a man who's often tongue-tied, George W. Bush is awfully good at double-talk. He has an annoying—and amazing—habit that follows a discernible pattern: He goes somewhere and touts some investment (often a Clinton-era creation) that the federal government makes to help America be smarter, safer and stronger. He praises the program, poses for pictures with the participants and gives a speech about how important the program is.

Then he goes home and cuts that program's budget. Look at the pattern and tell me if Dubya ain't the black widow of the federal budget:

KISS: **Bush Praised Volunteer from 'Even Start' Literacy Program.** During a speech, while in New Mexico on April 29, 2002, President Bush highlighted a local volunteer as an exemplary model of good citizenship. According to the *Albuquerque Tribune*, "Bush also will recognize Lucy Salazar, an Albuquerque mother and grandmother who tutors preschool and kindergarten students, according to a statement issued Friday by the White House. Salazar, a retired federal employee, also collects books for a reading program called Project Even Start, volunteers at her church, visits with residents at senior homes and hospitals, and is active with VSA Arts, an arts organization."[53]

DEATH: **Bush Proposed Cutting Even Start by 20 Percent.** President Bush's budget cut $50 million, or 20 percent, from Even Start funding in fiscal year 2003. New Mexico received $1,772,736 in Even Start funding this year (FY2002) and Bush's proposal would cut $344,580 from that state's funding next year.[54]

KISS: **Bush Visited Ethanol Plant, Discussed Energy.** On April 24, 2002, Bush traveled to South Dakota to support the campaign of Rep. John Thune (R-SD) for the Senate. During his trip, Bush visited the Dakota Ethanol Plant. Later in the day, during a GOP rally Bush voiced his support for ethanol. "There's plenty of room for ethanol in the energy mix in America. We must have it. We must have it for the good of our farm economy, we must have it for the good of our air. And we must have it for the national security reasons of the United States of America," Bush said.[55]

DEATH: **Bush Budget Eliminates $600,000 Grant for Dakota Ethanol Plant.** Bush's budget proposal eliminated funding for the United States Department of Agriculture (USDA) Bioenergy Program that provides grants to increase production of renewable fuels. The Dakota Ethanol Plant in Wentworth, SD—the very plant Bush visited—received $602,481.89 in FY2001 from the Bioenergy Program.[56] But under Bush's budget they can kiss that grant good-bye.

KISS: **Bush Visited the University of Pittsburgh to Tout Budget Initiative on Bioterrorism.** In February 2002, Bush traveled to the University of Pittsburgh Medical Center and spoke about his budget initiative to prepare for bioterrorism. "Part of homeland security is to have a first responders mechanism that's modern and current. And part of homeland security is to be prepared to fight any kind of war against bioterror," Bush said.[57]

DEATH: **Bush Budget Slashed Funding for Health Professionals by $278 Million; University of Pittsburgh Received Grants to Train Health Professionals.** In his FY2003 budget for the Department of Health and Human Services (HHS), Bush cut funding for health professionals from $388 million in FY2002 to $110 million, a 72 percent reduction. In 2001, the University of Pittsburgh Medical Center received two grants to train health professionals. One grant for $188,843 was allocated for Residency Training in Primary Care. The second grant for $254,882 was allocated in 2001 for Faculty Development Training in Primary Care.[58]

KISS: **Bush Visited Boys and Girls Club in Wilmington, DE, and Touted Mentoring.** On April 3, 2001, Dubya traveled to the H. Fletcher Brown Boys and Girls Club in Wilmington, Delaware. While there, Bush discussed the importance of funding mentoring programs. "I believe so strongly in mentoring. And I believe so strongly in helping children understand somebody loves them. And the government can't do that, but what the government can do is facilitate programs and allow faith-based programs to access federal monies so that they can help change hearts. . . . I viewed the Boys and Girls Clubs as faith-based programs, by the way, programs based upon the universal concept of loving a neighbor just like you would like to be loved yourself, and for that, I'm grateful," Bush said.[59] (Set aside the fact that Bush butchered the Golden Rule, and focus on the kiss.)

DEATH: **Bush Budget Eliminated $60 Million Grant to the Boys and Girls Club.** Six days after his trip to the Wilmington

Boys and Girls Club, Bush released his FY2002 budget, which cut funding for Boys and Girls Clubs of America by $60 million dollars. The cut eliminated a grant program allowing the Boys and Girls Clubs of America to operate programs for children in public-housing facilities in collaboration with state and local law enforcement officers.[60]

KISS: **Bush "Got Misty-Eyed" at Hospital Visit with Children Suffering from Cancer.** On March 1, 2001, after Bush submitted his budget blueprint, he flew to Egleston Children's Hospital in Atlanta to push his budget plan. At a leadership forum event, Bush praised the efforts of the doctors, nurses and parents. "This is a hospital, but it's also—it's a place full of love. And I was most touched by meeting the parents and the kids and the nurses and the docs, all of whom are working hard to save lives," Bush said. According to the *Atlanta Journal and Constitution*, Bush "got misty-eyed as [Vicki] Riedel, a 45-year-old mother from DeKalb County, recounted her daughter's battle with cancer."[61]

DEATH: **Bush Budget Cut Funding for Graduate Medical Education at Children's Hospitals.** Bush's FY2002 budget request cut funding for Children's Hospital Graduate Medical Education program by $35 million. This program provides grants to independent children's hospitals that train pediatric physicians. Under this program the Children's Healthcare of Atlanta at Egleston received a $553,732 grant in 2000.[62] He also cut, for the second year in a row, the Children's Hospital Graduate Medical Education Program, from which Egleston received a $3,635,111 grant.[63]

The Bottom Line

I am astonished when otherwise thoughtful conservatives accuse those of us who simply point to the impact of Republican economic policies on low- and middle-income Americans of waging class warfare. What on earth would you call cutting important programs that teach our children, train working people, protect employees on the job, so that we can send billions of dollars in tax cuts to the most fortunate among us? Why is it that the commentators and pundits—well-paid all, to be sure (I know; I'm one of 'em)—call criticizing Bush's war on working people a form of class warfare? Don't let them back you down. Nobody wants to punish success. No one wants to divide Americans. However, when our president proposes policies that yank the ladder of opportunity out from under those who are working to make it in order to give wads of cash to people who've already got it made, we have a duty to call it what it is: class warfare on behalf of the favored few and against most Americans.

I would respect Junior more if he were just honest with us. If he'd say, "Look, I don't think the government has any business subsidizing education, or college costs or job training." I wouldn't agree with him, but I'd respect his candor.

That's not how our president operates. In his desire to be a "compassionate conservative" (whatever that is), he gives speech after speech extolling the virtues of important government programs that help people. Then he cuts and guts the budget for those same programs when he thinks you're not looking.

Maybe it's all just political for him. But Bill Clinton, though a master politician, knew more than politics is at stake. Investing in people is about building a long-term, strong and sustainable economy. Who do you think drives those *fundamentals* that Bush and his economic team keep trying to tell us are so sound? The American people. Our productivity. Our skills. Our creativity. Our intelligence and our flexibility and our resourcefulness. All of those attributes are improved when we invest in our people. And they are all degraded when we turn away from those investments.

Sure, Dubya talks a good game, but on issue after issue he comes up short. In Texas, we'd say he's all hat and no cattle; all sizzle and no steak; all swagger and no stick; all windup and no pitch. You get the idea.

FIVE

The Best Environment
Money Can Buy

"First, we would not accept a treaty that would not have been ratified, nor a treaty that I thought made sense for the country."—George W. Bush on the Kyoto Treaty on Global Climate Change, 4/23/01.[1]

"And we need a full affront on an energy crisis that is real in California and looms for other parts of our country if we don't move quickly."—George W. Bush, press conference, 3/29/01.[2]

"There are some monuments where the land is so widespread, they just encompass as much as possible. And the integral part of the—the precious part, so to speak—I guess all land is precious, but the part that the people uniformly would not want to spoil, will not be despoiled."—George W. Bush, Media roundtable, Washington, D.C., 3/27/01.[3]

"The California crunch really is the result of not enough power-generating plants and then not enough power to power the power of generating plants."—George W. Bush, interview with the *New York Times* (1/14/01).

"Not since the rise of the railroads more than a century ago has a single industry [energy] placed so many foot soldiers at the top of a new administration."—*Newsweek* (5/14/01).

"When money determines who has access, it can determine whose interests are nourished."—*Houston Chronicle* editorial on the Bush–Cheney energy plan (5/28/01)

GEORGE W. BUSH HAS NEVER BEEN MISTAKEN FOR AN ENVIRONMEN-talist, but even a hard-core Bush critic would have been hard-pressed to predict just how savage Bush has been. No one actually *wants* pollution. No one—certainly no politician—sets out deliberately to poison the water or pollute the air. What happens is that other, more important, priorities get in the way. And, for George W. Bush, there is no more important priority than preserving, protecting and defending corporate power. "After elections, the payback begins," said Larry Noble, an analyst at the Center for Responsive Politics, a nonpartisan information house. "While this has occurred with every president in recent years, the problem is escalating."[4]

Bush's commitment to sucking up to the moneyed elite has even led the ol' Texas straight shooter to flat-out break a bunch of campaign promises.

Like Otter Said in *Animal House:*
You F----d Up; You Trusted Dubya.

While campaigning in Michigan on September 29, 2000, candidate Bush pledged that he would reduce four different emissions, including carbon dioxide: "We will require all power plants to meet clean air standards in order to reduce emissions of sulfur dioxide, nitrogen oxide, mercury *and carbon dioxide.*" (Emphasis added.)[5] Despite this campaign pledge, President Bush wrote to Republican senators to tell them he had decided to renege on his promise to regulate carbon dioxide emissions from power plants after encountering strong resistance from the coal and oil industries.[6]

He Broke Another Campaign Promise:
Not to Dump Nuclear Waste in Nevada

Nevada was a classic toss-up state in the razor-close 2000 presidential election. From 1972 through 1988, the state had gone Republican. Bill Clinton broke the GOP's hold, carrying it both in 1992 and 1996. Both Bush and Gore spent time and money there. Toward the end of the campaign, the state seemed to be swinging to Al Gore. The Gore campaign was accusing the Republicans of planning to locate the nation's high-level radioactive waste repository in Yucca Mountain, Nevada, despite some serious reservations from scientists.

The Bush-Cheney ticket responded by doing what it did best: misleading people. Earlier in the campaign, Bush had pledged that, "As president, I would not sign legislation that would send nuclear waste to any proposed site unless it's been deemed scientifically safe."[7] But the Democratic attack was having an effect. Gore, the environmentalist, was pointing to his long-standing skepticism about locating America's nuclear waste in Nevada, as well as the Bush-Cheney campaign's strong ties to its contributors in the nuclear industry.

So, Dick Cheney made a quick trip to Reno on October, 25, 2000—just days before the election—and declared: "They are distorting our positions to win votes. The fact of the matter is there isn't any difference between their position and the position of Governor Bush."[8]

The fact of the matter is that Cheney's promise—repeated in last-minute ads—allowed Bush and Cheney to carry Nevada by 21,597 votes out of 581,553 cast.[9] And, the fact of the matter is, if Bush and Cheney hadn't carried Nevada, no one would have ever heard of Katherine Harris or butterfly ballots in Florida.

And, the fact of the matter is, Bush and Cheney were not telling the truth to the people of Nevada.

Despite being urged by the General Accounting Office (GAO) to indefinitely postpone its decision to store nuclear waste in Yucca Mountain due to numerous unanswered technical and scientific questions, the Bush administration decided to dump all of America's nuclear waste in Nevada anyway. Campaign promises be damned.

This is serious stuff. Seventy-seven thousand tons of nuclear waste is going to be shipped, trucked and hauled by trains across the country to Nevada. It will travel through 43 states, coming within one mile of 50 million Americans. These "mobile Chernobyls" will be tempting targets for terrorists.[10]

Yucca Mountain is hardly an ideal site for thousands of tons of the most deadly stuff on earth—waste that will still be radioactive in a thousand years. Yucca Mountain is classified as a "Class 4–High Probability Earthquake Hazard Zone" by the United States Geological Service. There are 33 earthquake faults in the immediate area surrounding Yucca Mountain, including two that run under it. In 1992, an earthquake 35 miles away from Yucca Mountain measured 7.8 on the Richter scale.[11]

Why did Dubya and Dick Cheney break their word, go back on a campaign pledge, and dump nuclear waste in a place and by a method that may not be safe? I can't think of a single good reason.

I *can* think of 7 million bad ones. According to the Safe Energy Communication Council (SECC), an energy policy watchdog coalition of 10 national energy, environmental and public interest media organizations, the nuclear power industry contributed more than $7 million to the Republican Party during the 2000 election year.[12]

Corporations Pollute; You Pay

Chances are you've never created a toxic Superfund site. I'm just guessing here. We've never met and I never saw your college dorm room, but I think I'm on solid ground. Thanks to George W. Bush and the Republicans, even if you've never even generated a thimbleful of toxic waste, you're getting hit with the bill to clean it up.

The Bush administration refused to reauthorize the Superfund tax, which taxes corporations to pay for the cleanup of Superfund sites around the country. The Superfund tax, created in 1980 under the mantra *the polluter pays,* goes into a trust fund which is used to clean up *orphan sites,* where a responsible party could not be identified or could not pay. (It also pays for cleanups where the responsible party is recalcitrant, as well as in cases needing emergency action.) The Republican Congress let the corporate taxes—which finance Superfund cleanup—expire in 1995, and now the fund is running out of money.

Dubya has not called for reauthorizing the corporate taxes that support Superfund cleanups—taxes that chemical and oil companies had complained were a burden. So, guess who foots the bill now? Did you guess you, the taxpayer? *DING! DING! DING! Congratulations, you're our lucky winner. And here's what you've won: You get more toxic waste, fewer Superfund sites cleaned up, and more of your hard-earned tax dollars going to clean up toxic Superfund sites that you had nothing to do with creating. Thanks for playing the home version of YOU GET SCREWED! And now this word from our sponsors:*

In 1994, while the corporate polluters' tax was still in place, citizen-taxpayers only had to foot the bill for about 21 percent of Superfund cleanups. Since 1999, when the elimination of the corporate tax had drained much of the fund, that percentage has gone up to about 50 percent of the cost of cleanup.[13]

Although you're paying more, you're getting less. The cleanup of Superfund sites has declined under the Bush administration. More than 80 Superfund sites were cleaned up each year during the second term of the Clinton administration. In his first year in office, Bush's administration has cleaned up just 47, and it projects that number will fall to just 40 this year, and remain at 40 next year.[14]

If Kids Can't Handle a Little Arsenic in the Water, How Are They Gonna Learn to Drink Bourbon?

In March 2001, the Bush EPA announced it was overturning a rule from the Clinton administration that lowered the allowable level of arsenic in drinking water from 50 parts per billion (ppb) to 10 ppb.[15]

Now, arsenic is nasty stuff. Arsenic in drinking water causes cancer of the skin, lungs, bladder and prostate in humans. It has also been linked to diabetes, cardiovascular disease, anemia and disorders of the immune, nervous and reproductive systems, according to the EPA.[16]

It's not that Bush and the Republicans want more sick kids. Really, it's not. But, like the man said, "It's hard to see the light when your paycheck requires you to remain in the dark." And Dubya has gotten some very big checks from the forces of environmental darkness.

According to the Environmental News Network, activists who track such issues: "The Bush administration's recent abandonment of a plan to lower the amount of arsenic in U.S. drinking water appears suspect in light of a $5 million campaign contribution from the mining industry."[17]

"A lot of the waste dumped from mining operations contains arsenic," said Deanna White, deputy political director of the Sierra Club, "and Bush is letting them off the hook."[18]

As you may recall, there was an enormous outcry from Democrats, environmentalists and people who liked their bladders and prostates cancer free. So, because of the public pressure, the Bush administration buckled and returned to the Clinton standard.

If We Can't Get Arsenic in the Water, How About Raw Sewage?

A study by the Natural Resources Defense Council has some information that might make you think twice the next time you go fishing or swimming. According to the study, the Clinton administration issued long-awaited rules designed to limit the discharge of raw sewage into our water, and requiring public notice when sewage does overflow. The Bush administration blocked those rules—and all other Clinton rules—when it took office. But the Bushies have been in office a year and a half, and still no antisewage rule. Technically, the rule is still "under review," but environmentalists suspect that's just a ruse to kill it altogether.[19]

Of course, while the rules are suspended, raw sewage continues to flow straight into our water—without any public notice. It should go without saying, but in case President Bush is reading this, let me be clear: Raw sewage is, well, it's a bunch of crap. Literally. It causes gastrointestinal disorders, respiratory illnesses, and other diseases. It causes beach closures, fish kills, shellfish-bed closures and other environmental disasters. And, according to the EPA, sewage was discharged into our water some 40,000 times in the year 2000 (the latest year for which statistics were available).[20] All of which makes the Bushies' delay on this so outrageous.

I'm tempted to say, "Cut the crap," but that would be too easy.

Chew Your Air Carefully Now, It's Full of Carcinogens

Dubya then moved on to one of his favorite activities: trusting his campaign contributors—who happen to be corporate polluters—to keep the air clean.

Bush has laid waste to something called the New Source Review. Should you care? Well, that depends. If you breathe, you ought to care. If not, Bush's dirty air is no threat to you.

The Clean Air Act says that new power plants have to follow strict clean-air codes. Older plants are *grandfathered*; that is, they don't have to comply. But, as corporations modernize, expand, upgrade or replace older plants, those improvements—those new sources of power—have to be in compliance with the Clean Air Act.

Dubya's Environmental Protection Agency concluded that a Clinton-era enforcement initiative that used the New Source Review to force older power plants and refineries to reduce emissions should be scaled back. The Clinton initiative resulted in dozens of lawsuits against power plants that failed to comply with the Clean Air Act after making significant upgrades to their facilities. The proposed rollback in enforcement was a prelude to Bush's New Source Review proposal to relax enforcement of clean-air laws. "The White House is getting a lot of pressure from industry, especially power companies, to make changes . . ." in the New Source Review, said an administration official.[21]

On June 13, 2002, the Bush administration announced its proposed rule changes to New Source Review, which added up to what the *Washington Post* called "a major relaxation of clean-air enforcement rules." Bush's proposal would allow older utility and refinery executives to upgrade and expand their plants and increase their emissions without having to add antipollution equipment currently required by law. Bush's rules would effectively prevent future government legal action against violators of clean-air laws in all but the very worst cases of pollution. The proposal was a "major accommodation to officials of refineries and utilities" who had complained about aggressive enforcement policies during the Clinton administration.[22]

John Walke, an air-quality expert with the Natural Resources Defense Council, called Bush's New Source Review proposal: "The most sweeping and radical assault on a Clean Air program and environmental law enforcement since the inception of the EPA."[23]

Sen. James Jeffords, the independent senator from Vermont whose defection from the Republicans gave the Democrats control of the Senate, and who chairs the Senate Committee on the Environment and Public Works, said that Bush's New Source Review proposal was a "devastating defeat for public health and our environment" and threatened to subpoena administration officials and records involving the decision. The administration's proposal was "a victory for outdated polluting power plants and a devastating defeat for public health and our environment," Jeffords said.[24]

Bush's Head of Enforcement at EPA
Blows the Whistle on Dubya

The Bush-Cheney war on clean air has had one very important casualty already: Eric Schaeffer, the director of the Environmental Protection Agency's Office of Regulatory Enforcement. Schaeffer, a twelve-year veteran of the EPA, began his career under the first President Bush and had risen to director of enforcement. His efforts to pressure power-plant polluters into cleaning up their act were beginning to yield important results. And then came Dubya.

"In a matter of weeks," Schaeffer has written, "the Bush administration was able to undo the environmental progress we had worked years to secure. Millions of tons of unnecessary pollution continue to pour from these power plants each year as a result. Adding insult to injury, the White House sought to slash the EPA's enforcement budget, making it harder for us to pursue cases we'd already launched against other polluters that had run afoul of the law, from auto manufacturers to refineries, large industrial hog feedlots, and paper companies. It became clear that Bush had little regard for the environment—and even less for enforcing the laws that protect it." [25]

In his letter of resignation, Schaeffer didn't mince words. He said he was "fighting a White House that seems determined to weaken the rules we are trying to enforce. It is hard to know which is worse, the endless delay or the repeated leaks by energy industry lobbyists of draft rule changes that would undermine lawsuits already filed. At their heart, these proposals would turn narrow exemptions into larger loopholes that would allow old 'grandfathered' plants to be continually rebuilt (and emissions to increase) without modern pollution controls." [26]

This is not merely about one man's career. It's about your health. As Schaeffer noted in his letter of resignation, Bush is trying to weaken clean-air protections that literally save lives. Data supplied to the Senate Environment Committee by EPA last year estimate the annual health bill from 7 million tons of SO2 and NO2: more than 10,800 premature deaths; at least 5,400 incidents of chronic bronchitis; more than 5,100 hospital emergency visits; and over 1.5 million lost work days. Add to that severe damage to our natural resources, as acid rain attacks soils and plants, and deposits nitrogen in the Chesapeake Bay and other critical bodies of water."[27]

And, Schaeffer noted, enforcing the clean-air laws is cost effective, thus demolishing one of the Republicans' favorite myths. "EPA's regulatory impact analyses, reviewed by OMB, quantify health and environmental benefits of $7,300 per ton of SO2 reduced at a cost of less than $1,000 per ton. These cases should be supported by anyone who thinks cost-benefit analysis is a serious tool for decision-making, not a political game."[28]

So, according to one of the foremost experts—a man who was originally hired by George Bush Senior—enforcing our clean-air laws saves lives and is cost effective. And yet, Dubya's policy of cutting and gutting enforcement continues, propelled by the fabrication that industry will voluntarily clean up its own act. This is an outrage. Schaeffer's parting shot in his letter of resignation is a bull's eye: "Teddy Roosevelt, a Republican and our greatest environmental President, said, 'Compliance with the law is demanded as a right, not asked as a favor.' "[29]

In case you were hoping things have somehow gotten better since Schaeffer resigned in March 2002, consider what he wrote months later: "Behind the scenes, in complicated ways that attract less media attention (and therefore may be politically safer), the administration and its allies in Congress are crippling the EPA's ability to enforce laws and regulations already on the books. As a result, some of the worst pollution continues unchecked."[30]

The American Lung Association said the Bush proposal "will increase air pollution and threaten public health." They warned, "EPA is taking a page from Arthur Andersen's accounting 'cookbook' that will allow chemical companies, oil refineries, and power plants to increase air pollution while claiming on paper they are not."[31]

Bush has been so terrible on air quality that Jay Leno nailed him on it. "Last week," Leno said, "President Bush announced he's relaxing the clean-air standards. I guess choking once wasn't enough for him."[32] The audience roared. Leno also said: "President Bush is relaxing—they call it relaxing—the clean-air rules for utilities. He's claiming that this relaxing the clean-air rules will help the war on terrorism. The way it works is, all the extra smog will make it harder for terrorists to see our landmarks."[33]

Drill in the Wilderness

In a stunning suck-up to big oil, Bush has proposed opening up the country's protected land and national parks, including the Arctic National Wildlife Refuge, to oil drilling. In an interview with the *Denver Post*, Bush said his administration would look at "all public lands" for energy development.[34]

Next to tax cuts for the rich, drilling in the pristine Alaskan wilderness is Junior's favorite panacea. He—or other drilling supporters—have, at times, tried to sell it as a cure for the California energy crisis, as a remedy for the Bush recession, as a solution to our problems with Iraq, as the best way to help Israel, and as the best way to get health care to retired steelworkers.

Let's take these one at a time. First, the California energy crisis. The *New York Times* slam-dunked that one, writing in an editorial that "it is wholly specious to suggest, as Mr. Bush does, a connection between opening the refuge and California's energy problems. Less than 1 percent of California's electricity comes from oil. California's fuel of choice is natural gas, and if Mr. Bush wants to find natural gas, there are far better places than the coastal plain to look for it."[35]

How 'bout curing the Bush recession? Supporters of drilling in the Alaskan wilderness claim it would create 700,000 jobs. *Time* magazine says otherwise: "As for the 700,000 jobs, that number comes from an 11-year-old study commissioned by the American Petroleum

Institute that economists complain wildly inflates the employment potential. 'It's just absurd,' says Eban Goodstein, an economist at Lewis and Clark College, who predicts the real job growth will be less than one-tenth that number."[36]

But wouldn't drilling in the Alaskan wilderness make our problems with Iraq shrink? I've never understood that one. As CBS News reported, Bush "has cited Iraq's current oil embargo as proof that new drilling is needed more than ever."[37] Of course, we've had a boycott of Iraq since Junior's daddy was president—and we have allowed Iraq to sell oil, ostensibly for food, for years. But even supporters of drilling admit we won't see barrel one for eight to ten years.[38] By then Saddam Hussein will be dead or deposed or both, if we are to believe the bellicose promises of the Bush foreign-policy speeches.

If you're truly worried about America's dependence on unstable sources of oil (and who isn't?), the better course of action is not to sit around and wait ten years for the Alaskan oil to start flowing. According to a study by the American Council for an Energy-Efficient Economy, "Increasing the fuel efficiency of new cars and light trucks by just 5 percent a year would cut U.S. oil use by 1.5 million barrels per day within a decade. Over 40 years, such a program of increased vehicle efficiency would save 10–20 times more oil than the projected supply from the Arctic National Wildlife Refuge and more than 3 times total U.S. proven oil reserves today."[39]

Supporting Israel and helping retired steelworkers get health care have nothing to do with punching holes in the Alaska wilderness. But Alaska Republican Senator Frank Murkowski tried to round up votes for drilling by pledging to use the proceeds to pay the health-care costs of retired steelworkers or to provide aid to Israel.[40] In the end, senators decided that aid to steelworkers and Israel can stand or fall on their own merits, and drilling in the Alaskan wilderness went down to defeat.

After the Democrats in Congress stopped him from drilling in the Alaska wilderness, Dubya turned to the Rockies. The *Denver Post* reported the Bush administration had its sights set on such beautiful parts of the Rockies as: "the Powder River Basin in Wyoming and Montana; the Green River Basin in Wyoming and Colorado; the Uinta-Piceance Basin in Utah and Colorado; the San Juan-Paradox

Basin in Colorado, New Mexico and Utah; and the Montana Thrust Belt, also called the Rocky Mountain Front. And Agriculture Secretary Ann Veneman, who oversees the U.S. Forest Service, recently mentioned possible oil and gas development in the Lewis and Clark National Forest in the heart of the region. . . . In its budget for this year (the Department of the), Interior set aside $14 million for updates to land-use plans that are likely to increase energy production in natural areas like the Snake River area in Wyoming, the Colorado Canyon National Conservation Area and the Gunnison Gorge National Conservation Area."[41]

Don't Like Drilling? How 'Bout Mining on Public Lands?

Way back in 1872, when the government was looking to encourage settlement in the western part of our nation, Congress enacted a mining law intended to promote mineral exploration and development of federal lands. Miners were granted free access to the land and, if they got lucky and struck gold, they could stake a claim.

One hundred and thirty years have passed, but the laws that govern mining haven't changed much. Today, the mining companies, which extract billions of dollars of minerals from public lands, still don't pay federal taxpayers for that privilege. Former Chief of the U.S. Forest Service Mike Dombeck describes the 1872 Mining Law as "perhaps the most vexing and outdated natural resources law in the country." He explained: "The royalty provisions are simple: None exist. It is a blatant giveaway of public resources."[42]

Bruce Babbitt, the former Arizona governor who served as Secretary of the Interior under President Clinton, called the 1872 Mining Law "one of the most outrageous corporate subsidies" in America.[43] Babbitt thought that, at the very least, the federal government should alleviate the impact of some modern mining techniques—such as open-pit cyanide leaching—on the environment. So, the Clinton administration enacted new rules restricting mining, including one that gave the Bureau of Land Management the authority to deny permits for mining operations that would cause "substantial, irreparable harm" to environmental or cultural resources.[44]

Enter the Bushies. You already know how busy they were in those first weeks in office, what with breaking their campaign pledge to regulate carbon-dioxide emissions and lifting regulations that reduce arsenic in the country's drinking water. In March 2001, they took the country another step backward, announcing that they planned to suspend several other Clinton administration environmental initiatives, including the one that allowed the government to prohibit mining projects that would cause "substantial, irreparable harm" to the environment.[45]

The move stunned some: "We knew it was not going to be a great administration for us, but we didn't think it would be quite this bad either," said one shocked environmentalist.[46] Other conservationists had already figured the Bushies out; Dave Alberswerth of the Wilderness Society is one of them. He told the *Los Angeles Times*, "I think a consistent pattern is emerging here. Whatever the mining or coal or oil and gas industries want, they're going to get."[47]

Sadly, Mr. Alberswerth was right. The *New York Times* summed up the bad news: "The pendulum has swung significantly toward positions advocated by industry."[48]

In the 2000 election, donations from the mining industry to political candidates and parties had reached $6.5 million, with 86 percent of the donations going to Republicans.[49] Just weeks into the Bush administration, the return on that investment was unmistakable. Denise Jones, a lobbyist for mining companies, exulted that the Bush administration moves would "allow many [mining] operations to expand."[50]

More than a year has passed since those dark early days of the Bush administration, and those who'd hoped that the worst might be over after that initial barrage of antienvironment assaults have since been disillusioned. The Bush administration continues its dirty work for the mining corporations, just recently overturning a Clinton moratorium on new mining activity in an area of southwest Oregon known for its extraordinarily rich fish and plant life. (The new plan would only protect 117,000 acres of the 1 million acre tract protected by the Clinton administration.)[51]

"[The mining] industry thinks it has an absolute right to grind up mountains and poison streams and wreck the landscape," Bruce Babbitt once raged.[52] Think about that the next time you see Bush out there on Earth Day, dressed in plaid and grinning for a photo op, or maybe just remember the words of Charles Wilkinson, a law professor at the University of Colorado: "No question about it, industry has a straight shot at the public lands now."[53]

Fishermen and hunters, hikers and backpackers, campers and vacationers, were all angered by Bush's plans to turn our protected lands into oilfields and mines. The oil companies and mining operations that contributed to him in record numbers loved it. Junior may have his flaws, but he is one loyal politician. Not necessarily to the people who voted for him, who had no idea he'd attack precious public lands but to the corporate campaign contributors who serve as the Board of Directors of Bush, Inc.

Calling a Halt to Saving Public Land

In May 2001, the Bush administration declared a moratorium on new proposals for expanding the national park system, supposedly to clear up the backlog of park maintenance. Even many Republican members of Congress criticized this move. During the presidential campaign, Bush pledged to commit nearly $5 billion over the next five years to restore the nation's national park system, but his budget provided only $439.6 million for the first fiscal year. Rep. Joel Hefley (R-CO), chairman of the House Resources Subcommittee on National Parks, Recreation and Public Lands, said, "I applaud your trying to eliminate the backlog, but having only appropriated $500 million for fiscal 2002, it's going to take an awfully long time to eliminate that backlog."[54]

Bush promised $5 billion over five years, yet delivered less than one-tenth that in his first budget. That means one of two things is true: Either Bush is going to go on a national parks spending spree the likes of which we haven't seen since Teddy Roosevelt, or (and this is gonna shock you) Bush was fibbing. Again.

Wetlands Preservation Promise?
What Wetlands Preservation Promise?

In still another backtrack from a campaign pledge, Bush proposed relaxing a series of rules designed to restrict development and degradation of thousands of streams and other wetlands. According to the *Washington Post*, "Environmentalists complained that the proposal would undercut President Bush's pledges to preserve wetlands, making it easier for developers and coal mining companies to dig them up and fill them in."[55]

The Bush-Cheney Energy Task Force

There may be no other single activity that more perfectly exemplifies the Bush-Cheney administration than the Bush-Cheney energy task force. It has all the hallmarks of Bush and Cheney: The process was secretive, special interests and campaign contributors crowded out the national interest, there was only the barest pretense of caring about the environment, and the final product was great for Enron and Exxon, but terrible for the environment.

What a contrast even to the last Bush presidency. When Poppy Bush set out to develop a national energy policy back in his administration, his energy task force had open proceedings and traveled to eighteen cities around the country. Junior's task force met behind closed doors for three months with industry lobbyists.[56]

The *Washington Post* described the process: "The Bush administration's energy task force is something of a secret society. At the start of each meeting with outside groups, task force members requested that the session be off the record. They said they will share no documents, to prevent the information from leaking. The members are expected not to talk to the media, and the few who do are not able to talk about policy."[57]

The director and activist Rob Reiner once noted that the Republican Party's idea of diversity was to have men from two different oil companies on the national ticket. When we heard that, most of us chuckled knowingly, but our laughter turned to anger when it became apparent just how utterly and completely the Bush administration is dominated by the energy industry. Consider this: the president, the vice president, the national security adviser, the secretary of energy, the secretary of the interior, the secretary of the army, the chairman of the National Economic Council, the White House chief of staff, the president's chief political adviser, the vice president's chief of staff, the director of presidential personnel, and numerous lesser officials—all either came from the energy industry, owned stock in the energy industry or did legal or lobbying work for energy-related industries. No wonder *Newsweek* declared uncategorically: "Not since the rise of the railroads more than a century ago has a single industry placed so many foot soldiers at the top of a new administration."[58]

And as if dominating the administration were not enough, the energy industry contributed more than $48.3 million to the Republicans for the 2000 elections.[59]

And, man, did the Bushies ever deliver for their corporate patrons. "The energy [plan] was so favorable it almost seemed like power companies got everything they . . . asked for," an economic analyst told the Associated Press.[60]

The meetings, outside participants, agenda, notes and minutes of these meetings are still being kept secret by the Bush administration, which is being taken to court by the General Accounting Office—the nonpartisan investigative arm of Congress. Never in its history has the GAO sued the White House.

Although many of the facts and details of how the Bush-Cheney task force operated are still being kept secret, the Center for Public Integrity has been able to compile a list—only partial and preliminary, to be sure—of key meetings with one very major, very special interest: Enron. Many of these meetings, the center found, coincided with major donations to the Republicans.[61] Was the fact that the meetings and the donations coincided just . . . a coincidence? Must be. After all, the Bushies were shocked that Hollywood heavyweights like Steven Spielberg got to sleep in the Lincoln Bedroom. Surely they would not sell America's energy policy to the highest bidder.

(For more on Enron, see Chapter 7.)

While Enron clearly got the most access, other special interests were not far behind. As the *New York Times* reported: "Interviews and task force correspondence demonstrate an apparent correlation between large campaign contributions and access to Mr. Cheney's task force. Of the top 25 energy industry donors to the Republican Party before the November 2000 election, 18 corporations sent executives or representatives to meet with Mr. Cheney, the task force chairman, or members of the task force and its staff. The companies include the Enron Corporation, the Southern Company, the Exelon Corporation, BP, the TXU Corporation, FirstEnergy, and Anadarko Petroleum."[62]

In case you're not taking notes, a pattern is emerging. The Bush-Cheney task force meets with a special interest. The special interest donates money. The Bush-Cheney task force report favors that industry. Ain't democracy grand?

The Bush-Cheney report is pro-big oil, pronuclear, procoal, pro-Enron, and propower plant. About the only things it isn't are proconsumer and proenvironment. No wonder the report itself was widely panned by those interests who were not deemed special enough by the Bush-Cheney White House—interests like clean water and clean air and reducing toxins. As one of those not-very-special interests, the Natural Resources Defense Council, concluded: "At best the energy industry has undue influence on major governmental decisions that will affect all Americans. At worst, the energy industry, which is enjoying record profits, has hijacked our government and now has the power to seriously weaken environmental safeguards, threaten public health and gouge consumers." [63]

The Bottom Line

All the Ralph Nader–voting, Birkenstock-wearing, Green Party goofballs are probably gagging on their granola right now. And well they should be. Their stupid, self-absorbed, infantile infatuation with Nader allowed Bush to win and, if not to win, at least to get close enough to steal it. Without Ralph Nader helping Bush, Al Gore would have handily won New Hampshire and Florida, which would have given him an electoral college victory of 295–242. And you would never have heard of chads, or butterfly ballots or Katherine Harris.

More important, you would never have heard of the Bush-Cheney environmental wrecking crew. So, the next time you hear some smug lefty say there's not a dime's worth of difference between the two parties, ask him (or her) about arsenic in the water, toxins in the air, nuclear waste in Nevada—and on your highway. Ask about taxpayers paying to clean up Superfund sites instead of corporations, about plans to drill in the national wilderness, mine in the national parks, log in the national forests. Ask about protecting wetlands, preserving public lands, and fighting global climate change. Ask about special interest lobbyists and corporate fat cats making environmental and energy policy behind closed doors. Then ask her (or him) if they're going to play that little game of "Vote Green; Elect Republicans" again, because it's your life, your health, your air, your water and your planet they're playing with.

SIX

Crime in the Suites:
How the Republicans Told
Corporate America "Anything Goes"

"Not that I can think of."—House Republican Whip Tom DeLay, when asked if there were any federal regulations he would choose to keep.[1]

"Clearly it's not business that needs more regulation—but government itself."—Rep. Newt Gingrich.[2]

"[The GOP takeover of the House] represented a triumph for business, a form of political revenge for the multinational corporations and small businesses who now found themselves full partners of the Republican leadership in shaping congressional priorities."[3]—David Maraniss and Michael Weisskopf, *Tell Newt to Shut Up.*

"The [Bush] White House has been supporting Senator Phil Gramm's efforts to stop reform of accounting and corporate reform on Capitol Hill."—Lou Dobbs, *Moneyline,* CNN.[4]

"The Bush administration on the issue of corporate governance is about as compromised as the Clinton administration was on marital fidelity. You have issues that are going to come home to roost again and again."—Professor Jack Coffee, Columbia University School of Law, a leading securities regulation scholar.[5]

Dubya: You're No TR

The greatest Republican president of the twentieth century, Theodore Roosevelt, would be mighty pissed. The man who supported campaign finance reform legislation back in 1905—calling for banning corporate contributions for political purposes[6], would not approve of the money machine George W. Bush has turned the Republican Party into.

Nor would TR countenance for a minute the extraordinary influence corporate special interests have today in his old party. At the beginning of the twenty-first century, as at the beginning of the twentieth, Teddy Roosevelt would be railing again on behalf of what he dubbed "the little man" against the "malefactors of great wealth."[7] Sounds like a hotter, more populist version of Al Gore's "people versus the powerful," doesn't it? No wonder the GOP—and a few pusillanimous, proplutocrat Democrats—are so frightened of it.

No, the man who busted the trusts, who pressured coal companies to respect their miners, who created the federal departments of Commerce and Labor, who used the power of the federal government to rein in the railroads and who gave us such big government, regulatory regimes as the Pure Food and Drug Act and the Meat Inspection Act would not be happy today.[8]

George W. Bush is no Teddy Roosevelt. Oh, sure, there are superficial similarities. Both were the scions of old-money eastern establishment families; both educated at Harvard (where Bush got his MBA); each a Republican who became president after serving as governor of his state. But, as I said, all that is superficial. What is more interesting is that both served as president at a time when enormous concentrations of wealth produced equally enormous concentrations of political power. Roosevelt knew which side he was on, and the history of the twentieth century was more prosperous and more productive—as well as more fair—because TR stood for "the little man."

The question before us at the beginning of the twenty-first century is whether W's presidency will signal a similar revolution—but this time we're looking at a counterrevolution. Will the history of the twenty-first century be marked by greater and greater power in the hands of fewer and fewer people—or will latter-day TRs rise up to ensure that a strong America is strong for all of us?

The Republican Revolution of '94

George W. Bush rode the Republican Revolution of 1994 into the governor's mansion in Austin. Meanwhile, the leaders of that revolution in Washington were planning to do what successful insurgents have done for centuries: sack and loot the capital. When the British took Washington in 1814, they burned the White House. When the Republicans seized power in 1994, they set out to do more permanent damage.

On March 12, 1995, the *Washington Post* published a lengthy front-page story detailing the astonishing and brazen extent to which corporate interests had taken control of the Republican Congress. At the center of the takeover was Tom DeLay. Mr. DeLay, the congressman who represents the area where I grew up, on the Gulf Coast of Texas, is not a conservative. He's a kook. He got into politics after being in the pest control business. Tom DeLay hates the government. He hates regulation. But he loves, loves, loves DDT.

So, you can imagine how angry Tom was when the federal government banned DDT. DDT, you may recall, was one of the nastiest, most noxious insecticides. It came into use after World War II, first for mosquito control, later as a general insecticide. But insecticides, like other nasty things, roll downhill. The DDT got into the water, so it got into fish, which in turn were eaten by bald eagles—America's symbol since 1782.[9] DDT made the eagles' eggshells too thin and, so, the bald eagle population, once more than 100,000 nesting pairs in 49 states (not Hawaii), had, by 1963, dwindled to just 417 pairs.[10]

In 1972, the Environmental Protection Agency banned the use of DDT in the United States. Within a quarter century, the bald eagle was off the endangered species list, and thriving in virtually every state in the union.[11] If that seems like a happy ending to you, you don't know Tom DeLay.

Tom DeLay is not a happy man. He is an angry man. He says DDT is perfectly safe and the bald eagle was never in danger. And he says the EPA is "the Gestapo of government."[12]

Now, I like invective as much as the next guy. Actually, more than the next guy, but this is a little over the top. For those of you who slept through either World War II or your history class, a refresher course, courtesy of the Simon Wiesenthal Center:

"The Gestapo was the secret state police of the Third Reich, led by Hermann Goering. After 1938, the Gestapo became the main instrument of anti-Jewish policies, and special units were trained to terrorize and Nazify foreign countries. The Gestapo was considered above the law and served Hitler in remaking the world in the Nazi image." [13]

Okay, so maybe Tom's rhetoric goes a little over the top. But haven't we all compared dedicated public servants, whose job it is to keep our air and water clean, with the worst Nazi mass murderers in history? No, actually, we haven't.

And DeLay's record actually backs up his rhetoric. When the Republican Party swept the congressional elections of 1994, DeLay launched a blitzkrieg attack against regulations of all sorts, especially targeting any regulations that protect citizens from the excesses of corporate power. He was asked in those heady days of early 1995, in the first weeks after the Republicans took power, if there was a single federal regulation he would keep. His answer was unwavering: "Not that I can think of." [14]

Not a single federal regulation would Tom DeLay keep. Not the protections of our food supply and our water supply. Not the federal regulations and mandates that ensure our cars don't blow up and our planes don't crash. Nor the regulations that ensure that our medicines are safe and effective, our air is clean and our children are safe.

You've got to hand it to DeLay: he's no slacker. He worked assiduously to write his radical vision into reality. He organized something called "Project Relief," which the *Washington Post* said, "sounded more like a Third World humanitarian effort," [15] than what it was—a coalition of lobbyists who moved into the Capitol and, at Tom DeLay's behest, took over the House of Representatives. DeLay assembled 350 different special-interest lobbyists—every polluter and corporate rip-off artist you could imagine. They came with their checkbooks wide open. According to one study by the Environmental Working Group, political action committees associated with the lobbyists in Project Relief had donated more than $10 million to House candidates in 1993–94. [16]

They got an amazing return on their investment: They got to run the House of Representatives. The *Washington Post* reported that "the roles of legislator and lobbyist blurred"[17] as lobbyists actually wrote legislation and handed it to Republican members of Congress, who dutifully introduced it and voted for it. The lobbyists wrote "talking points" for the Republicans; the Republicans took them on the House Floor and read them. The lobbyists even had something very few congressmen have: an office in the Capitol building itself.[18]

Alexander Hamilton once pointed to the Capitol and told a visitor with pride: "Here, sir, the people govern."[19] You can almost imagine Hamilton spinning in his grave, as DeLay seems to proclaim that now, sir, the lobbyists govern. And DeLay was unabashed about it. He told the *Washington Post* that it made sense to let lobbyists write laws instead of the duly elected members of Congress because, he said, "they have the expertise."[20] The lobbyists were just as up front and honest about what they were doing, and for whom. One petrochemical lobbyist told the media, "I'm not claiming to be a Boy Scout. No question I thought what I was doing was in the best interest of my clients."[21]

How the GOP Congress Fostered the Current Corporate Scandals

Much of what DeLay's forces passed in the House was blocked by Senate Democrats or President Clinton. However, the Republican Congress was able to use its power to block President Clinton from enacting needed reforms that might have prevented many of the corporate abuses that have cost so many people their jobs and so many more their investments. They included:

Republicans Went after the SEC from Day One. In the first months of the Republican revolution, House GOP leaders reportedly instructed Reps. Dan Frisa and Jack Fields "to ease regulations of stocks, bonds and mutual funds, undermining laws that have been a cornerstone of investor confidence for more than 50 years."[22] News accounts from the time report that Republicans solicited Wall Street firms for advice on how to diminish the SEC's influence.[23]

Republicans Made It Harder to Hold Corporate Crooks Accountable. One of the planks in the GOP's Contract with America was the Private Securities Litigation Reform Act, which shielded corporations and accountants from certain shareholder lawsuits. President Clinton vetoed the bill, and his reasoning was prescient. He said that he was not "willing to sign legislation that will have the effect of closing the courthouse door on investors who have legitimate claims. Those who are the victims of fraud should have recourse in our courts. . . . our markets are as strong and effective as they are because they operate—and are seen to operate—with integrity. I believe that this bill, as modified in conference, could erode this crucial basis of our markets' strength."[24] The Republican Congress overrode Clinton's veto—the only time it did so in his presidency.

Abner Mikva, one of the living legends of the law, is the only person I can think of who has held top positions in all three branches of government. He was a leading member of Congress from Illinois, then served as a federal judge on the D.C. Circuit Court of Appeals (one step below the U.S. Supreme Court), then served as White House counsel under President Clinton. Judge Mikva, reflecting on the Private Securities Litigation Reform Act, has written: "Simply put, Congress reduced the incentives against committing fraud. . . . By inhibiting the rights of individuals to seek damages, we lowered the risks for securities fraud, eliminated deterrence, and fostered a culture of laxity. . . . The effect was to remove many of the restraints on corporate officials and their accountants."[25]

Lynn Turner, former chief accountant for the SEC agreed: "The chance of getting sued has been reduced. . . . Private lawsuits have a much greater impact, even [more] than the SEC, on the behavior of company executives and auditors."[26]

Republicans Blocked the Clinton Administration from Separating Auditing from Consulting. President Clinton's Securities and Exchange Commission Chairman Arthur Levitt wasn't called the "champion of the small investor" for nothing.[27] In 1998, he warned the country about the potential for corporate book-cooking, saying, "Today, American markets enjoy the confidence of the world. How many half-truths, and how much accounting sleight-of-hand, will it take to tarnish that faith?"[28]

When Arthur Levitt proposed a rule that would have set new standards to ensure that auditors are independent—by barring the built-in conflict that occurs when the same firm serves as an auditor for a company it's also consulting for—he decried "a massive conflict of interest between accountants' duties as auditors and the profits they earn as consultants to the same corporate clients."[29] This was *a big deal*, Levitt said. "Nothing less than the public interest is at stake. If investors cannot trust the sanctity of the numbers, our markets lose their credibility."[30]

The Republican Congress, not to put too fine a point on it, freaked out. Rep. Michael Oxley, the chairman of the House Financial Services Committee, called the Levitt-Clinton proposal "a Draconian solution to a perceived problem."[31] Oxley joined Rep. Billy Tauzin, the powerful Louisiana Republican who chairs the House Energy and Commerce Committee, and Rep. Thomas Bliley of Virginia, chairman of the House Commerce Committee, in writing what the *New Republic* called an "extraordinary" letter with a "not-very-veiled threat."[32] The trio of Republican congressional committee chairmen formed a phalanx to protect the accounting lobby, even threatening hearings on how the SEC was doing its job."[33] A total of 48 members of Congress wrote Levitt to protest his reform, including Sen. Phil Gramm, chairman of the Senate Banking Committee (whose wife was the chair of the audit committee at Enron).[34]

The GOP heavyweights killed the Levitt-Clinton reform by threatening the budget. As Levitt has said, "As we got down toward the end of the congressional session the threats were made, 'Arthur, if you go ahead with this proposal, it is likely that a rider will be placed upon your appropriations bill which says the SEC will not be funded if they proceed with the issue of auditor independence.' "[35] In fact, both the House Republican leadership and the Senate Banking Committee (again, chaired by the senator from Enron) had drafted just such a rider.[36]

And so, the Levitt-Clinton auditor independence reform was killed by the Republicans. And the corporate scandals came. And the Republicans are to blame. Am I overstating it? Not according to the experts. Lynn Turner, the former chief accountant for the SEC, said, "If these reforms had been in place earlier, we would not have had an Enron."[37] *Business Week* presciently described Levitt's fight: "A powerful regulator, fiercely convinced he's acting in the public interest, charges that the $70 billion industry—upon which the entire financial system depends for reliable corporate reports—has been

It's Clinton's Fault

One of the most amusing things to watch in Washington these days is the right-wing blowhards trying to blame President Clinton for the wave of corporate crime that's been sweeping America. As these pages prove, the record is clear: President Clinton and his administration fought the Republicans from the first day to the last to prevent corporate rip-offs. And, as more than one expert has said, had Clinton's reforms been enacted, there would have been no Enron.

So, stymied by the facts, the right blames Bill Clinton's philandering for corporate America's lawlessness. As he often does, Lardbutt Limbaugh makes the case: "Who taught us how to get around laws? A, Ronald Reagan. B, Bill Clinton. Who taught us how to have his way with words and women? Who taught us, my friends, how to lie under oath and get away with it? Who taught us that oral sex isn't sex, and now kids across the country in grade school try it out?"[38]

Since it was on the radio, I can't promise you he got through this with a straight face. But let's pretend for the sake of argument that Lardbutt meant it. The logic goes like this: Once Clinton became the first man in the world to cheat on his wife, the decent men of Corporate America were so shaken, so rocked, so scandalized that they decided to loot their companies, cheat their investors and rip off their workers.

Man, that was one powerful b.j.

As Peter Beinart pointed out in the *New Republic,* to suggest that corporate swindlers became greedy because Clinton was amorous, you'd have to believe that Ivan Boesky and Michael Milken, who pillaged in the Age of Reagan, "lost their moral bearings because the Gipper was a divorcé who neglected his children."[39]

Still, foam-at-the-mouth Clinton haters (like the *Wall Street Journal* editorial page) argue, Clinton should be responsible be-

★ ——— ★ ——— ★ ——— ★ ——— ★ ——— ★ ——— ★ ——— ★

cause, as president, he set the moral climate. "It's impossible to understand Enron," the *Journal* pontificated, "outside the moral climate in which it flourished . . . the Clinton years, when we learned that 'everybody does it.' " Okay, Beinart replies, if we're going to blame Clinton's sin for corporate criminality, don't we have to give Clinton credit for everything that went right morally in America under his watch? When Bill Clinton was in the White House teen pregnancy fell 22 percent. The crime rate fell to its lowest levels in a generation. Welfare rolls were cut by nearly half. Divorce, abortions, teen suicides, unwed pregnancies—they all fell under Clinton's moral tutelage.

Clinton's private sinfulness notwithstanding, he and his administration worked tirelessly to protect us from corporate crooks, while the Republicans did everything but drive the getaway car for the bandits. Maybe that's why they want to blame it all on Clinton getting to "third base" (or whatever it is) with a young woman. I'll tell you this: If I had to choose my sinners, I'd rather my president be in bed with a young woman than with Enron.

corrupted by its search for growth. Levitt's challenge will echo long after he has left Washington."[40]

Organizing and orchestrating the opposition to the Levitt-Clinton proposal was Mister Big himself, the powerful lawyer and lobbyist for the accounting industry, Harvey Pitt.[41] Pitt, of course, was rewarded for blocking this reform by being appointed by President Bush and Vice President Cheney to chair the Securities and Exchange Commission. And foxes everywhere who dreamt of guarding henhouses smiled.

Republicans Hamstrung the SEC Budget. House Republicans voted to cut the SEC budget every year from 1996 through 2001.[42] This occurred at a time when stepped-up enforcement efforts by the Clinton administration and increased business activity due to the Clinton boom increased the volume of the SEC's workload by 350 percent.[43] As the General Accounting Office—the watchdog arm of

Congress—reported, "The SEC's workload and staffing imbalances have challenged the SEC's ability to protect investors and maintain the integrity of securities markets."[44]

Arthur Levitt pressed for a salary increase for SEC staff to "keep a cop on every beat." In a letter to House and Senate leaders, Levitt said that with salaries rising on Wall Street and at law firms, the SEC "simply cannot pay our staff enough to keep them. . . . Since 1994, we have been experiencing an alarming rate of turnover." Levitt pushed for pay parity, to put SEC salaries on par with those of banking agencies, and to counter the overall 13 percent attrition rate of SEC staff in 1999 and the fact that only 46 percent of the SEC's open positions were filled that year.[45]

Despite the GOP's constant efforts to undermine reform, the Clintonistas pressed on. In 1998, the SEC established an Earnings Management Task Force to review the filings of companies whose financial statements raised suspicions. As a result, more than 50 companies were forced to revise their financial statements or earnings releases, and another 40 needed to correct the timing of recognition for revenues or other costs. Restatements by high-profile companies such as Rite Aid were prompted by these reviews.

Chairman Levitt also established the Financial Fraud Task Force, a talented group of enforcement lawyers and accountants dedicated to investigating possible fraud. In September 1999, the SEC announced the filing of 30 enforcement actions against individuals and companies for financial fraud. Major enforcement cases were brought against companies and their executives and auditors, including W. R. Grace, AOL, Microstrategy, PricewaterhouseCoopers LLP and KPMG LLP. PricewaterhouseCoopers paid a $2 million penalty because half its partners were found to have violated existing conflict of interest regulations—the first such penalty against a major international accounting firm. Chairman Levitt's SEC also initiated cases against Waste Management, Sunbeam, Microsoft, and Rite Aid—key cases that revealed how major companies were manipulating their books and misleading their shareholders.[46]

Republicans Ended Regulation of Enron's Energy Derivatives and Blocked Clinton's Efforts to Regulate Them. Congressional Republicans in 2000 added to the omnibus appropriations bill language that deregulated energy trading—specifically exempting energy contracts from oversight, as well as exempting online trading.[47] The *Wall Street Journal* reported that the "provision was sometimes referred to by Capitol Hill staff as the 'Enron Point.' "[48] *USA Today* noted that "two powerful Republicans from Texas, Reps. Dick Armey and Tom DeLay, were instrumental in pushing the legislation through the House."[49]

Lest we allow Armey and DeLay to get all the credit, consider how the Nader-created group Public Citizen described the role played by the senator from Enron:

> Phil Gramm spearheaded a successful effort to bury major commodity deregulation legislation in an appropriations bill that was introduced during the chaotic days after the Supreme Court issued its ruling sealing George W. Bush's victory in the disputed 2000 presidential election. . . . Operating a commodities exchange with no transparency and no accountability, Enron was able to command far more market share than before Gramm's legislation. In the days after the law took effect, California was plunged into a month-long nightmare of rolling blackouts. Phil Gramm's drive to remove government oversight of Enron's operations is to blame.[50]

Here, again, the Clinton administration has I-told-you-so rights. Back in 1997, Clinton's chair of the Commodities Futures Trading Commission, Brooksley Born, proposed greater disclosure of energy derivatives. Jim Leach, the Iowa Republican who chaired the House Financial Affairs Committee at the time, called a hearing and called Chairwoman Born on the carpet.[51] And, just to make sure the reform proposal stayed dead, Republican Representatives Robert Smith of Oregon, Larry Combest of Texas and Tom Ewing of Illinois introduced legislation blocking the CFTC from increasing scrutiny of energy derivatives.[52]

And, in 2000, as Senator Gramm was trying to slip his Enron legislation through, William Rainer, Brooksley Born's successor as chairman of the Commodity Futures Trading Commission, told Congress he was "deeply concerned" about a bill to exempt energy trading from CFTC review, noting that those who trade energy derivatives were not subject to any other oversight. Rainer's objections were largely ignored by the Republican-controlled Congress, and the exemption, heavily backed by Enron, became law.[53]

How the Republicans Fought for the Tax Evaders, Money Launderers and Pension Raiders

The GOP record of crippling reform is sad, but its record of affirmatively trying to help corporate special interests avoid their duty to pay taxes and play by the rules you and I have to follow is truly sordid. Here's a brief summary of what they did to aid some of the worst corporate practices.

Republicans Defended Corporate Benedict Arnolds

It's one thing to be wrong in hindsight—to have lacked Brooksley Born's prescience about the need to regulate Enron. It's another altogether to flat out side with corporations that thumb their nose at their patriotic duty.

No one likes to pay taxes. And yet, at the end of the day, the revenue the government takes in pays the salaries, buys the equipment, provides the training and purchases the arms for the military that keeps us free; taxes support the whole infrastructure of freedom in addition to national defense, allowing us to bite into a burger without worrying about dying, or give our children a drink of water from the tap without worrying about them getting sick. So, when huge corporations evade their fair share of the burden of providing for the common defense and promoting the general welfare, those flag-waving patriots in the Republican Party become incensed, don't they?

Think again. It was the Clinton administration that first tried to crack down on these corporate traitors. As co-chairman of the Forum on Harmful Tax Practices of the Organization for Economic Cooperation and Development (the major industrial nations), Clinton Treasury Secretary Larry Summers led an effort to increase transparency and curb special tax deals offered by countries to lure multinationals and allow corporations like Kenny-Boy Lay's Enron, Dubya's Harken Energy and Cheney's Halliburton to hide some of their profits from U.S. tax collectors. We're not talking about chump change here. An estimated $70 billion each year are lost to the Treasury in nontransparent offshore tax havens.[54]

Rather than being outraged that the good ol' U-S-of-A is being cheated out of $70 billion by these Benedict Arnolds, the Republicans defended the traitors. Republican House leaders Dick Armey and Tom DeLay—the best butlers a billionaire ever had—were quick to defend their corporate patrons, writing Summers hot letters and blasting the OECD rules as "harmful to tax competition."[55] Tax competition? No, it's tax avoidance, Dick. And it's unpatriotic.

When Dubya took office his Treasury Secretary, Paul O'Neill, abandoned the Summers-Clinton effort, telling a congressional committee he did so because, "I was troubled by the notion that any country, or group of countries, should interfere in any other country's decisions about how to structure its own tax system. I felt that it was not in the interest of the United States to stifle tax competition that forces governments—like businesses—to create efficiencies."[56]

You see? It's not about protecting what legendary New York prosecutor Robert Morganthau estimates is $800 billion stashed in the Caymans alone—twice as much as is in every bank in New York and equal to 20 percent of all the money deposited in all the banks in America.[57] It's not about helping a tiny number of the wealthiest people and corporations avoid paying their fair share of taxes. It's not about the disloyal, unpatriotic economic traitors who get rich off America's freedom, stay safe because of America's military strength, enjoy the blessings of liberty, but don't want to pay for it. No, say Dubya and O'Neill and the rest of Bush, Inc. No, it's about "tax competition."

Right.

Republicans Opposed Clinton Crackdown on Money Laundering

After September 11, all Americans realized that a key element in the war on terrorism is stopping the terrorists' ability to finance their operations. President Clinton and his administration understood that long before most Americans had ever heard of Osama bin Laden or al-Qaeda. That's why President Clinton sent legislation to Capitol

Hill that would have given the Treasury Secretary the power to bar foreign countries and banks from access to the American financial system unless they cooperated with money-laundering investigations. Republican Senator Phil Gramm, then chairman of the Senate Banking Committee, held up the bill.[58] When the Bush administration came in, cracking down on money laundering was no longer a priority. Secretary O'Neill told the *Wall Street Journal*, "The government has not been respectful of the cost it imposes on society." Apparently, Mr. O'Neill is more respectful of Mr. bin Laden and his money. Bush's National Economic Council chairman Larry Lindsey was equally protective of the money launderers' rights.[59]

Of course, the Bush administration did come out strong for locking the barn door after the horse had escaped. On September 19, 2001—just days after the 9/11 attacks—the administration changed its tune. As the *New York Times* reported: "Since last week's attacks, proposals to curb money laundering by terrorists have suddenly gained support among old opponents—including the Bush administration—after languishing for two years . . . Led by its chief economic adviser, Lawrence B. Lindsey, the administration did not want to pressure international banks in the United States and elsewhere to open their books."[60]

Republicans Watered Down Democrats' Attempt to Protect 401(k)'s

In 1997, former stockbroker and Democratic Senator Barbara Boxer became worried that companies were loading their employees' 401(k)'s with company stock, which could be catastrophic if the company went under. So, she introduced the "401(k) Pension Protection Act of 1997," which was intended to protect workers' retirement nest eggs by making it illegal for companies to invest more than 10 percent of a worker's 401(k) pension fund in company stock or other risky investments. Once the Republicans in the Senate (who ran the place back then) got through with it, Boxer's great idea had been defanged. One securities publication reviewed it this way:

> The new law limits the investment of new contributions to 401(k)s in employer stock to 10%. However it does not apply to the employer match. Nor does it apply if plan

participants have any discretion in how their plan assets are invested. Nor does it apply if the 401(k) plan is supplemented by a defined benefit plan or some other form of retirement plan. In other words, *regulators will be hard-pressed to find a plan to which the Boxer limit on employer stock will apply.* . . . (Emphasis added.)

But watering down the Boxer legislation was a big mistake, says Ruth Hughes-Guden, a principal with Morgan Stanley Asset Management in New York, and the director of the firm's defined contribution business. "The Boxer bill was a very good idea," she states. "We now have an inordinate level of stock-specific risk in the industry. Look out when one of these stocks goes down.[61]

Ms. Hughes-Guden—and Senator Boxer—were prescient. Too bad the Repubs didn't listen to them.

Republicans Wanted to Allow Corporations to Raid Pension Funds

In 1995, the Republicans in Congress slipped a section into the mammoth budget bill—the Omnibus Budget Reconciliation Act of 1995—to allow corporations to raid their workers' pension funds by greatly reducing pension protections that the Democratic Congress had passed back in 1990. The Joint Committee on Taxation estimated that, under the GOP provision, corporations would have withdrawn $30 to $40 billion from their workers' pension funds.[62] President Clinton vetoed that version of the Republican budget. You can bet that if Dubya had been in the White House, he'd have signed that thing faster than he can say "subliminable."

Mister Bush Comes to Town

When George W. Bush came to the White House, the right-wing Republican congressional leadership knew they had the front man they needed. Dubya fit into their plans perfectly—giving a veneer of decency to economic policies that can only be described as savage.

Of course, I didn't have high expectations to begin with, but even

I was surprised at how Bush began his presidency. First impressions matter. They set the tone for an entire presidency. The first piece of legislation Bill Clinton signed into law was the Family Medical Leave Act—a terrific law that has enabled tens of millions of Americans to take a little time off to care for a sick relative or welcome a new baby into the world. (And, by the way, it didn't seem to drag our economy down, as the right-wingers predicted. Turns out we can have a decent society and a strong economy at the same time.) The first piece of legislation George W. Bush signed into law as president was a right-wing special-interest law to repeal workplace-safety protections. After more than a decade of study, the Labor Department had issued rules protecting working men and women from repetitive stress injuries and other on-the-job injuries. The Occupational Health & Safety Administration estimates the worker-safety rules would have prevented 460,000 musculoskeletal disorders a year— disorders that cost employers $15 billion to $18 billion a year in workers' compensation costs.[63]

Some employers, no doubt, do a good job of protecting their employees. They now will be at a competitive disadvantage. Being a good corporate citizen doesn't pay when the White House is controlled by people who think protecting steelworkers and secretaries from on-the-job injuries is a bad idea.

Bush Opposed Corporate Fraud Bill He Was Forced to Sign

Dubya may have started with repealing health-and-safety rules, but he didn't stop there. In fact, he was just getting warmed up. His aversion to policing corporate behavior, apparently, runs deep. Even in the wake of the accounting scandals and the alleged rip-offs from Enron, WorldCom, Xerox, Tyco and all the rest, Junior and his administration dug in their heels as long as they could, stalling, pooh-poohing, and generally opposing Democrats' efforts at real reform. The Democratic bill, sponsored by Maryland Senator Paul Sarbanes, was perhaps the toughest set of new corporate accountability rules since the creation of the Securities and Exchange Act of 1934. Many thoughtful observers and experts saw Sarbanes, one of the most cerebral and least partisan members of the Senate, as the right man with the right ideas at the right time.

President Bush, however, was not one of those thoughtful observers. His Treasury Secretary, Paul O'Neill, criticized Sarbanes's bill, warning the Senate to "avoid hastily constructed reforms that will have harmful unintended consequences."[64] O'Neill elaborated on his skepticism of the corporate reforms, saying, "We will never be able to write rules that anticipate every possible subterfuge."[65]

Bush and Cheney themselves were more than a little leery about any corporate reform with teeth. According to the *Washington Post*, "Officials said Bush and Vice President Cheney were adamant that they not hurt the economy by imposing too much regulation.... One official said that as some of the harsher proposals were examined, it was decided that they would be ineffective or have unintended consequences."[66]

There are those "unintended consequences" again. Whether intended or not, the consequences of the Republican mania for deregulation and their blind worshiping of corporate special interest is a $7.4 trillion loss in the equity investments of the American people.[67] Seems to me they ought to be more concerned about the obvious consequences of their *laissez-faire*, procorporate religion.

Even the administration's top cop on corporate crime, SEC Chairman Harvey Pitt, was more interested in hanging around the (metaphorical) donut shop than arresting the bad guys. Following Enron's collapse, ol' Harvey said, "I have said many times already that I do not believe new legislation or new regulations are the key to solving every problem." Pitt said he opposed a "one-size-fits-all" formula dictating which consulting services an auditor may engage in. Following the WorldCom collapse, Pitt reiterated his reluctance to support real reform, saying, "The problem with writing things in stone, however, is that legislation is very difficult to pass and undo. The Glass-Steagall Act, passed in 1933, took 65 years to get rid of."[68]

Congressional Republicans, too, opposed elements of the stronger, Senate Democratic version of corporate accountability legislation. "There are some major flaws in the Senate bill," said Rep. Mike Oxley (R-OH), the House Republicans' leader on such issues. Oxley, like the Bush administration, was particularly concerned that the new regulatory body would oversee auditors.[69]

Senate Banking Committee Ranking Member Phil Gramm (R-TX), working with the accounting industry, delayed consideration of the Sarbanes bill by more than one month. According to *CQ Weekly,* "On the morning of May 16, Sen. Phil Gramm assembled a team of lobbyists to help him minimize, if not stop outright, new regulation of the accounting industry in the aftermath of Enron. 'It was a classic Gramm rally-the-troops' session, said one of the lobbyists who participated. The gist of the Texas Republican's exhortation, this lobbyist said, was that the representatives of the accounting industry and several business trade associations needed to execute a simple strategy: 'Stall, stall, stall.' The lobbyists obliged Gramm's call. . . . The American Institute of Certified Public Accountants, the industry's main trade association, orchestrated a letter-writing campaign among its members . . . while the U.S. Chamber of Commerce blanketed the Senate with an opposition message." Gramm criticized fellow lawmakers for writing a "one-size-fits-all prescription when clearly that one size does not fit all."[70]

In the end, of course, the good guys won. Public pressure—from citizens, shareholders and the many honest businessmen and women who wanted real reform—was too much even for the Bush-GOP-special interest coalition. Both the Senate and the House ultimately passed legislation that was at least as strong, if not stronger, than Senator Sarbanes's original Democratic bill.

Nearly every Republican voted for it, and President Bush signed it in the East Room of the White House. Often when major legislation is to be signed, the president uses the Rose Garden to do it. White House aides said the July heat moved them indoors. I'm not so sure. It may have been July on the calendar, but when George W. Bush signed a major piece of corporate reform legislation, I'm pretty sure hell was freezing over.

Meet the New Boss, Same as the Old Boss

One of the cosmetic attempts Dubya has made to appear tough on corporate crime was to appoint a special multiagency task force on corporate corruption. Its chairman, Deputy Attorney General Larry Thompson was, in the words of the *Washington Post,* "a director of a credit-card company that paid more than $400 million to settle allegations of consumer and securities fraud."[71]

Seems that Mr. Thompson was a board member and chairman of the audit and compliance committee for Providian Financial Corporation. Now, Providian is one of those upstanding corporate citizens that makes its money from what's called the *subprime* credit market.[72] That is, they target poor people with lousy credit ratings. Critics call this "predatory lending." Providian called it damned profitable.

While Thompson was on the board Providian paid a staggering $400 million to settle charges that it had, according to the *Post*, "inflated its financial results by charging excessive fees and engaging in other practices that state and federal officials said broke consumer protection rules."[73] It is important to note two things: First, the alleged wrongdoing took place while Thompson was helping to run the company as a board member. Second, even though the company shelled out 400 million clams, it did so while neither admitting nor denying wrongdoing.[74]

Because he was called to public service in the Bush-Ashcroft Justice Department, Thompson cashed out his stock for millions. A few months later, after disclosing problems with defaults in its credit card portfolio, the stock collapsed and the fine folks at Providian laid off thousands of employees.[75]

The Bottom Line

There is nothing—nothing—America's first CEO president and his fellow Republicans won't do for corporate special interests. And it will never end—so long as corporate special interests have money and Republicans have power. Think I'm wrong? Check out this entreaty from Tennessee Republican Senator Bill Frist. The Senate's only doctor and reputed to be a truly decent man, Frist wrote a letter to corporate lobbyists at the height of the corporate scandals. He asked them for campaign cash, and told them that if the Republicans regained control of the Senate, they would "relax the stranglehold of rules, regulations and restrictions on American business."[76]

The Republican right can try to blame Clinton, but that's like an arsonist blaming the fire department. He and his administration did everything in their power to protect us from the slimeballs in the suites, while the Republicans did everything in their power to aid and abet the rip-off artists. Here's a handy checklist to remind you of who were the good guys and who were the bad guys in the great corporate rip-off of 2002.

- Clinton and the Democrats tried to ensure auditor independence by banning accounting firms from being both auditor and consultant at the same time; led by Harvey Pitt, the Republicans blocked the reform.

- Republicans passed the Private Securities Litigation Reform Act, which made it easier for corporate swindlers to avoid being held accountable. President Clinton vetoed it, saying, "those who are the victims of fraud should have recourse in our courts."[77] Republicans—with some Democrats—overrode Clinton's veto.

- Clinton Commodities Futures Trading Commission Chair Brooksley Born proposed greater regulation of derivatives. Her proposal was beaten back by House Republicans, including then-House Banking Committee Chair Jim Leach (R-IA).

- William Rainer, Born's successor as chairman of the Commodity Futures Trading Commission, told Congress he was "deeply concerned" about a bill to exempt energy trading from CFTC review, noting that those who trade energy derivatives were not subject to any other oversight. Rainer's objections were largely ignored by the Republican-controlled Congress, and the exemption, heavily backed by Enron, became law.

- Clinton Treasury Secretary Larry Summers proposed a crackdown on tax havens, such as those used by Enron, and money-laundering practices used by Osama bin Laden and others. His proposal was opposed by the GOP Congress. When the Bush administration took office, Treasury Secretary Paul O'Neill abandoned Summers's crusade, and embraced tighter controls on money laundering only after 9/11.

- Sen. Barbara Boxer (D-CA) proposed banning investment of more than 10 percent of the total 401(k) plan in the employer's stock—the maximum that investment experts recommend a person sink into *any* company. The GOP Senate watered down her bill so much it didn't apply to virtually any corporation in America.

SEVEN

Bush, Inc.:
A Wholly Owned
Subsidiary of Enron

"Enron didn't receive any special treatment . . . Did we talk to energy companies? Absolutely. You'd have to be a damn fool to put together a comprehensive, nationwide energy policy and not talk to energy companies."—Vice President Dick Cheney, NBC *Nightly News with Tom Brokaw* (1/28/02).

"He was a supporter of Ann Richards in my run in 1994." —President George W. Bush on ex-Enron CEO Ken Lay, remarks to the press, the White House (1/10/02).

"I was very close to George W. and had a lot of respect for him, had watched him over the years, particularly with reference to dealing with his father when his father was in the White House and some of the things he did to work for his father, and so [I] did support him."—Ken Lay, on how and why he supported Bush over Richards in 1994, PBS *Frontline* (3/27/01).

"Cheney, when he was putting his energy policy together, met I guess six times with Enron, 'cause their advice, you know, was so good."—Al Franken, *Politically Incorrect,* ABC (1/15/02).

OF ALL THE CORPORATIONS THAT GEORGE W. BUSH AND HIS FELLOW Republicans suck up to—and believe me, there are a lot of them— one corporation stands out. One enormous corporation has the hubris, the arrogance, the lust for power, the desire for money and the contempt for the rules and those who play by them to make it the perfect match for George W. Bush.

Enron.

Dubya and Enron's CEO, Ken Lay—to whom Junior was so close he dubbed him "Kenny-Boy," and sent him scores of warm, personal letters—are birds of a feather. That's why George's behavior after Enron collapsed was so disconcerting. Said to prize loyalty above all other virtues, the president pretended he barely knew Kenny-Boy. Dubya tried to tell reporters that Lay had been a supporter of Governor Ann Richards when Bush ran against her in 1994. It's an important point. Or, it would be—if it were true.

A Patron of the Art of Politics

In point of fact, Enron was the single largest patron of George W. Bush's improbable political career. Think about that. Of all the corporations that have dumped money on Bush (the all-time champion of raising special-interest corporate cash), not one gave Bush more than Enron.

Ken Lay donated $122,500 to his campaigns for governor, and Enron was a "Gold" sponsor for both of Bush's gubernatorial inaugural committees—a designation that cost a total of $100,000.[1]

And, when Dubya decided to run for president, Kenny-Boy was there again. Enron gave $1,328,290 in total to Bush and the GOP, and Lay himself was a Bush Pioneer, raising at least $100,000 for the Bush presidential campaign. Lay was also a co-chairman of an April 2000 RNC gala tribute to Bush, meaning that he raised or contributed at least $250,000 for that event.[2]

As a presidential candidate—and, later, during the infamous Florida recount, Bush found Enron's corporate jet useful.[3]

Of course, like any politically sophisticated corporation, Enron gave to both parties, but it wasn't exactly balanced. In the 2000 election cycle, Enron donated $152,139 to Democratic candidates running for federal office. By contrast, in that same cycle Enron contributed $1,324,315 to George W. Bush's presidential campaign, the Bush-Cheney Recount Committee, the Bush-Cheney Inaugural Committee and the Republican National Committee.[4]

In other words, George W. Bush alone received more than nine times more money from Enron than every Democrat running in every House and Senate race in America *combined*. Staggering.

The mutually beneficial relationship between Kenny-Boy and Junior went beyond the normal contributor-politician situation. The intertwined fates of Enron and its wholly owned subsidiary Bush, Inc. is a remarkable story.

Howdy, Pardner: Bush's 1986 Business Deal with Enron

Bush's association with Enron predates his time as governor. Bush's oil company was a partner of Enron in an oil well back in 1986. At the time, Bush's firm was known as Spectrum 7, and it was in trouble. The *New York Times* says it "was struggling to stay afloat during a collapse in the world oil prices."[5]

Enron rode to the rescue. Although Enron had only been formed in 1985 (by the merger of Houston-based Houston Natural Gas and Nebraska-based InterNorth), within a year it was in business (or as we say in Texas, "bidness") with George W. Bush. The well drilled by the Enron-Bush partnership struck oil and gas, but not much. The partners may not have even recouped their investment.[6] Nothing sleazy about that. But it does show the hypocrisy, the jaw-dropping mendacity of the man who sat in the Oval Office and pretended he barely knew Ken Lay as Enron spiraled into bankruptcy.

Was Dubya a Lobbyist for Enron?

There is something sleazy, however, about the story of how George W. Bush once served as a lobbyist for Enron. In 1989, the Argentine newspaper *La Nacion* reported that George W. Bush had met that year with Rodolfo Terragno, who was the Minister of Public Works and Services in the government of President Raúl Alfonsín. *La Nacion* said they met in Argentina to discuss oil investments.[7]

Nothing much came of the story until Dubya was elected governor of Texas. Then, in November 1994, the *Nation* (a crusading American progressive magazine) did some reporting on Junior's business activities and came across the Argentina story. *Nation* Washington editor David Corn, a respected journalist, spoke with

Terragno, who was by then a Member of the Argentine Chamber of Deputies. What Terragno told Corn sounds an awful lot like influence peddling.

Terragno said he received a telephone call from Dubya. The son of the vice president of the United States of America was calling the Argentine minister of public works and services to pressure him, in the words of the *Nation*—"to award a contract worth hundreds of millions of dollars to Enron, an American firm close to the Bush clan."[8]

Indeed, Terragno was responsible for making multimillion-dollar decisions concerning a proposed pipeline across Argentina to ship natural gas to Chile. Enron, as the largest gas pipeline outfit in the U.S., might have been a good candidate for the construction job, except for the fact that—in typical arrogant Enron fashion—it had seriously alienated the minister. Seems Enron was already pressing the Argentine state-owned gas company to sell gas to Enron at a very low price. What's more, Terragno told the *Nation*, Enron's proposal for the multimillion-dollar pipeline deal was only one-half-page long.[9]

Terragno was angry. Enron was on thin ice.

That's when, according to Terragno, Dubya jumped into the mess. Terragno says Dubya called him, introduced himself as the son of the vice president of the United States, and made clear that he thought the pipeline—with Enron building it—should go through.[10]

"He tried to exert some influence to get that project for Enron," Terragno recalled in an interview with the *Nation*. "He assumed that the fact he was the son of the [future] president would exert influence . . . I felt pressured. It was not proper for him to make that kind of call."[11]

Dubya did not say whether he was working for Enron, or what his connection to the pipeline deal might have been, but Terragno got the message that the pipeline and Enron were important to the Bush family.[12]

The *Nation* can pick up the story from here:

> Shortly after Terragno's conversation with George W., more Bush-related pressure descended on him, the former minister claims. Terragno says he was paid a visit by the

U.S. Ambassador to Argentina, Theodore Gildred. A wealthy California developer appointed ambassador by President Reagan, Gildred was always pushing Terragno to do business with U.S. companies. This occasion, Terragno notes, was slightly different, for Gildred cited George W. Bush's support for the Enron project as one reason Terragno should back it. "It was a subtle, vague message," Terragno says, "that [doing what George W. Bush wanted] could help us with our relationship to the United States."

Terragno did not OK the project, and the Alfonsín administration came to an end in 1989. Enron was luckier with the next one. The pipeline was approved by the administration of President Carlos Saúl Menem, leader of the Peronist Party and a friend of President Bush."[13]

When the *Nation* tried to ask Junior about this in 1994, he refused to be interviewed. He did, however, respond to written questions, and his answers were curious yet categorical. The *Nation* wanted to know if Bush had ever spoken to Terragno about the pipeline deal, and whether Dubya had had any sort of business relationship with Enron.[14] Bush basically said, "I did not have business relations with that corporation, Enron."

What he literally said—or rather, wrote—was: "The answer to your questions are no and none. Your questions are apparently addressed to the wrong person."[15]

Hmmmm. What does that mean? Does it mean that perhaps Terragno had been snookered? That someone else, pretending to be Junior, had called Terragno? No, that wouldn't explain why—according to Terragno—the American ambassador had expressed an interest, and had raised the name of Vice President Bush.

Enron, too, issued a denial: "Enron has not had any business dealings with George W. Bush, and we don't have any knowledge that he was involved in a pipeline project in Argentina."[16]

Now, we know the first part of that statement is false. Enron, in fact, had a business deal—and, by all reports, an honest one—with Dubya back in 1986. As for the second part, what do they mean "we don't have any knowledge that he [Bush] was involved in a pipeline project in Argentina"? Enron, as its unfortunate investors and employees learned, is a master of obfuscation. And it sure muddied the waters here.

Who Needs a Lobbyist When You Have the Governor?

While the question of whether George W. Bush ever lobbied for Enron remains unanswered, there is no doubt that Bush served as a lobbyist—albeit one paid by the taxpayers of Texas—for Enron while he was governor. According to archives of their correspondence, Kenny-Boy wrote his friend George scores of times, asking for favors great and small.[17] He was rarely told no.

For example, at the request of Ken Lay, then-Governor Bush placed a call to then-Governor Tom Ridge of Pennsylvania concerning the deregulation of the electricity market in Pennsylvania. Pennsylvania was seen as a stepping-stone for Enron, which continued to grow in influence as an energy broker and supplier.[18] On October 17, 1997, Lay wrote Bush, "I very much appreciate your call to Governor Tom Ridge a few days ago. I am certain that will have a positive impact on the way he and others in Pennsylvania view our proposal to provide cheaper electricity."[19]

The *Philadelphia Daily News* reported that, "Enron seemed to get most of what it wanted in Pennsylvania. The electricity market was opened up for competition, and Enron's stock price continued to soar."[20] The Pennsylvania Public Utility Commission member who cast the deciding vote in favor of freeing up the electricity market was Nora Brownell, whom Lay later pressed President Bush to appoint to the Federal Energy Regulatory Commission. Bush did. The Pennsylvania governor whom Bush phoned to lobby on behalf of Enron, Tom Ridge, is now Bush's Director of Homeland Security.

Dubya was, of course, more than happy to help Enron within the borders of Texas as well. In 1999, Bush signed a bill into law that allowed corporations whose power plants were not covered by the Clean Air Act—including Enron—to continue to pollute Texas's air. The Bush bill did this by merely *asking* companies to "voluntarily" reduce their emissions, as opposed to imposing mandatory restrictions. The law that Bush signed (SB 766) did not mandate that companies clean up their air pollution, but it did increase the fees they must pay if they continue to pollute. Environmentalists estimated that only eight or nine grandfathered companies—out of more than 800—were likely to reduce emissions because of the legislation. Without a legal requirement to clean up their act, the corporations made a cold, calculated decision: It was cheaper to pollute (and pay the fees) than to clean up.

In 1995, Enron emitted 2,166 pounds of "grandfathered" polluted air into Texas. "The responsibility for the failure of the Texas Legislature to pass legislation closing the grandfather loophole and achieving necessary clean air benefits for Texas rests with George W. Bush . . . The governor chose to placate his polluter friends and contributors rather than move more aggressively against grandfathered polluters," said Ken Kramer, director of the Sierra Club.[21]

Take Me Out to the Ball Game

When Dubya decided to embark on his quest for the White House, the Lay–Junior relationship kicked into high gear. Lay raised money by the truckload, and Bush rewarded him with the most precious commodity a politician has: his time. On April 7, 2000, George W. Bush was one of the busiest men in America. He had just crushed John McCain in the Pennsylvania and Wisconsin primaries, and was beginning to plan his vice presidential selection process.[22] But Dubya took time out from the busiest year of his life to go to a baseball game.

This was no ordinary baseball game. This was the opening of Enron Field, the taxpayer-subsidized stadium for which Enron had purchased the naming rights. Despite the fact that Bush was the certain Republican nominee for president, and the sitting governor of Texas, he did not throw out the first pitch. His buddy Ken Lay did, with Dubya cheering him on. Perhaps as a consolation prize, Kenny-Boy did throw a private party for Junior at his ballpark.[23]

The (Enron) Ties That Bind

Once he claimed the presidency, George W. Bush paid back Kenny-Boy's many favors in spades. He populated the government of the United States of America with Enron cronies. According to the people at the website *The Daily Enron* (www.dailyenron.com), who've been tracking the Enron scandal from Day One, "52 former Enron executives, lobbyists, lawyers or significant shareholders" were placed in key positions of Bush, Inc.[24]

Every new president gives some plum political jobs—ambassadorships and the like—to his political supporters. But Dubya gave the Enron gang real power. Consider this list of just some of the top Bush officials with close Enron connections:

Assistant to the President Karl Rove. Widely thought to be the most powerful staffer in the West Wing, Rove held Enron stock worth between $100,000 to $250,000 while the administration was writing its energy plan.[25]

Chairman of the National Economic Council Lawrence Lindsey. Had earned $50,000 from Enron for consulting services.[26]

Chief of Staff to Vice President Dick Cheney Lewis "Scooter" Libby. Was an Enron stockholder.[27]

Secretary of the Army Thomas White. A former vice president of Enron. He oversaw Enron's bidding for the privatization of army utilities. News reports say White has pushed for greater privatization of army utilities.[28] White has been criticized by Democratic Senator Carl Levin and Republican Senator John Warner for not revealing the full extent of his Enron holdings, and for allegedly failing to divest his Enron holdings as he had promised the Senate Armed Services Committee he would do.[29]

White has also been criticized by other senators, including California Democrat Barbara Boxer, for the scores of contacts he had with his former Enron colleagues after he became secretary of the army. White insists the contacts were all innocent.[30]

·U.S. Trade Representative Robert Zoellick. A member of Enron's Advisory Council. When Zoellick visited India as trade representative in July 2001, he was asked about Enron's Indian interests. Zoellick explained that he was on Enron's Advisory Council and excused himself from participating in any discussion on the subject. "So, I don't talk about Enron."[31]

Commerce Department General Counsel Theodore W. Kassinger. Was an Enron consultant.[32]

Maritime Administrator William G. Schubert. Served as an Enron consultant.[33]

Undersecretary of State Charlotte Beers. Held between $100,001 and $250,000 of stock in Enron when she was nominated by Bush.[34]

Undersecretary of Commerce Grant Aldonas. Also disclosed owning between $15,001 and $50,000 of stock when he was nominated.[35]

Other Bush administration officials who owned stock in Enron when they were nominated include Defense Secretary Donald Rumsfeld, Undersecretary of Agriculture Thomas Dorr, Undersecretary of Commerce Kathleen Cooper and the Director of the White House Office of Science and Technology Policy John Marburger.

To be sure, it would be unfair to say that any of these public servants were necessarily compromised by their Enron ties. It may be that none of them were. But it is remarkable that one company—one very corrupt company—had so many ties to so many Bush administration officials.

Toe the Enron Line or Hit the Road

One thing is certain: when Kenny-Boy asked Georgie Junior to jump, Bush was already in the air before he asked "How high?" Lay served on the Bush transition team, and interviewed candidates for the Federal Energy Regulatory Commission, the federal regulators with oversight over Enron's core business—electricity grids and gas pipelines.[36]

In an interview with the Public Broadcasting System, Lay was up front about his influence, describing how he gave Bush his hand-picked list of acceptable FERC regulators. "I brought a list, we certainly presented a list," Lay said. "As I recall, I signed a letter which in fact had some recommendations as to people that we thought would be good (FERC) commissioners."[37]

Can you imagine that? Bush asked Enron's CEO to tell Bush who should be regulating Enron? Imagine, if you will, that you're a bit of a leadfoot. You like to speed, and you're pretty sure you're going to be facing a judge in traffic court someday. How much easier would you sleep at night if you got to appoint the judges?

Clay Johnson, head of White House personnel, could not name another company aside from Enron that had sent him a list of preferred candidates for FERC.[38]

It was a sweet deal, and Lay made the most of it. Two of the names on Kenny-Boy's approved list, Patrick Henry Wood of the Texas Public Utility Commission and Nora Brownell of the Pennsylvania Public Utility Commission, were ultimately nominated by Bush to the FERC.[39]

Wood's nomination to chair the FERC has generated the most controversy. He replaced Curtis Hebert Jr., a protégé of Mississippi Republican Senator Trent Lott. Wood was known as a supporter of market-oriented regulation of utilities, very much in line with Enron's hands-off regulatory attitude. Hebert, while a conservative Republican, had long opposed Enron's approach on certain issues. The *New York Times* reported that Lay "offered him a deal: If [Hebert] changed his views on electricity deregulation, Enron would continue to support him in his new job."[40]

Specifically, the *Times* reported, Lay wanted Hebert to support a national push for retail competition in energy and opening of access to the electricity grid to companies such as Enron. Hebert told the *Times* he refused the offer. 'I was offended,' he recalled, though he said he knew of Mr. Lay's influence in Washington and thought the refusal could put his job in jeopardy."[41]

The price of disagreeing with Kenny-Boy was high—even for a Trent Lott Republican. Hebert told CNN that Lay had told him, "he and his company, Enron, could no longer support me as chairman."[42]

So, in a power play that was audacious even by the standards of Washington, Pat Wood replaced Curtis Hebert. And Ken Lay was a happy man.

The Bush-Cheney Task Force for Enron . . . err . . . Energy Policy

Choosing its own regulators was just the beginning of the influence Enron wielded over Bush-Cheney, Inc. Federal regulators disclosed to Senator Barbara Boxer of California that Enron's highly paid lobbyists and other corporate executives had at least 25 meetings and phone calls with 19 energy regulators—all in less than a year.[43] The contacts ranged from dinners to tours of Enron's trading floor in Houston to more detailed conversations about Enron's desire to deregulate markets in a way that benefited Enron.[44]

Whatever Lola Wants, Lola Gets.
(Only this time, Lola's name is Enron.)

Crusading Democratic Congressman Henry Waxman of California has produced a remarkable report that meticulously documents all the provisions in the Bush-Cheney energy task force report. It should be required reading for every right-wing dunderhead who claims Enron got nothing from the Bush administration. Consider these helpful recommendations:

- **Open Access to Electricity Transmission Facilities.** Enron described this as its "single most important initiative."[45] This would allow Enron and other energy traders to have access to the power transmission lines of electric utilities. The Bush-Cheney energy task force embraced Enron's position, even though critics see it as an expansion of federal regulatory control over state control.[46]

- **Repeal of the Public Utility Holding Company Act of 1935.** Enron wanted this New Deal reform law repealed so it could own more than one electric utility. The Bush-Cheney energy task force embraced Enron's position, although consumer groups opposed it.[47]

- **Federal Eminent Domain for Siting of Transmission Facilities.** Enron wanted to expand its electricity grid by siting facilities where Enron thought they were necessary, even if states opposed them. The Bush-Cheney energy task force embraced Enron's position, despite the opposition of the (largely Republican) Western Governors' Association, which saw the issue as a federal power grab, eroding states' control over where power-transmission facilities could be located.[48]

- **Expansion of Transmission Facilities.** Enron wanted to expand the nation's electricity transmission facilities. The Bush-Cheney task force embraced Enron's position.[49]

- **Federally Owned Transmission Facilities.** Enron wanted access to the transmission assets of federal facilities like the Bonneville Power Administration in the Pacific Northwest or the Tennessee Valley Authority in the Southeast. The Bush-Cheney task force embraced Enron's position.[50]

- **Uniform Interconnection Procedures and Standards.** Enron wanted the federal government (by way of the newly Enron-friendly FERC) to establish interconnection procedures and standards for new power plants, so that all new plants could connect to the national electricity grid in a uniform fashion, which would make it easier for Enron to get access to power from any new plant in the country. The Bush-Cheney task force embraced the Enron position.[51]

- **Incentive Rates for Transmission Facilities.** Enron wanted new rates to allow transmission facility owners to collect additional profits—above a normal rate of return—for investments in the transmission system. The Bush-Cheney task force embraced the Enron position, despite the fact that the American Public Power Association called incentive rates "unnecessary," and said they "will certainly lead to higher costs for consumers."[52]

- **Comprehensive Electricity Restructuring Legislation.** Both Ken Lay and his successor as CEO, Jeffrey Skilling, had testified before Congress (back before they were both taking the Fifth) in favor of comprehensive energy restructuring legislation. The Bush-Cheney task force embraced Enron's position, despite the strong opposition of consumer groups.[53]

- **Establishment of a National Transmission Grid.** Kenny-Boy called this proposal "a highway for interstate energy in electricity." The Bush-Cheney task force embraced Enron's position, despite testimony from the Southern Company (a major electrical utility) that "It does not make sense—from either an economic or reliability standpoint."[54]

- **Promoting an Energy Derivatives Market.** About 90 percent of Enron's revenue (back when it had revenue) came from energy trading. Thus, promoting an energy derivatives market was a high priority for Lay, Skilling and Company. The Bush-Cheney task force embraced Enron's position.[55]

- **Emissions Credits.** Enron sought a global market in which to trade carbon emissions credits under a global climate change agreement. While it opposed the Kyoto Protocol on Global Climate Change, the Bush-Cheney task force did embrace Enron's call for "market-based incentives, such as emissions trading credits to help achieve the required reductions" in CO_2 levels.[56]

- **Expedited Permits for Energy Projects.** Enron owned pipelines, coal power plants, hydroelectric power plants, natural gas power plants, and more. It argued that the permitting process was too expensive and cumbersome. The Bush-Cheney task force embraced Enron's position.[57]

- **Expanded Natural Gas and Oil Drilling.** Enron strongly supported increased drilling for oil and gas. The Bush-Cheney task force embraced Enron's position, recommending at least seven different steps the federal government should take to promote such drilling.[58]

- **Support for Energy Projects in India.** Enron owned a majority interest in a $2.9 billion natural gas plant in Maharashtra, India, which had been embroiled in a nasty dispute. The Bush-Cheney task force embraced Enron's position, calling on the Secretary of State to "work with India's Ministry of Petroleum and Natural Gas to help India maximize its domestic oil and gas production."[59]

• **Increased Support for U.S. Energy Firms Abroad.** Enron was involved all over the world—from the Caribbean to Asia, Europe and the Middle East. The Bush-Cheney task force embraced Enron's position, leaning on the secretaries of state, commerce and energy to support U.S. energy firms abroad.[60]

• **Promotion of Wind Power.** Now here's one you'd think he-men like Junior and Cheney would scoff at, but Enron strongly supported a tax credit for wind power. The Bush-Cheney task force embraced Enron's position, recommending an extension of the tax credit.[61]

• **Hydropower Relicensing.** Enron owned four hydroelectric plants, which held federal licenses that were due to expire within five years. Enron wanted to simplify the relicensing procedures. The Bush-Cheney task force embraced Enron's position.[62]

Perhaps the most infamous example of Enron dictating America's energy policy is the extraordinary influence it had in the supersecretive Bush-Cheney energy task force. Now, that task force was dominated by corporate interests, so being the most influential corporation in that forum is kind of like being the tallest guy in the NBA. You've got some serious competition.

The *Financial Times* reported that "Mr. Lay—a close friend of the Bush family for years—is thought to be the only executive to have a private meeting with Vice-President Dick Cheney when he was formulating the new president's energy policy."[63]

The *New York Times* says Lay's influence reached beyond even snagging the sole solo meeting with Cheney. "Lay also had access to the team writing the White House's energy report, which embraces several initiatives and issues dear to Enron. The report's recommendations include finding ways to give the federal government more power over electricity transmission networks, a longtime goal of the company that was spelled out in a memorandum Mr. Lay discussed during a 30-minute meeting earlier this spring with Mr. Cheney. Mr. Cheney's report includes much of what Mr. Lay advocated during their meeting, documents show."[64]

In all, according to Cheney's office, the task force met at least six times with Enron executives or representatives.[65]

Rep. Henry Waxman (D-CA) is the ranking member of the House Committee on Government Reform. He and his staff analyzed the Bush-Cheney energy task force's final recommendations, matched them against Enron's lobbying desires, and found out that Enron had won the lottery. According to Waxman, no less than 17 specific policy proposals from the Bush-Cheney energy task force would have benefited Enron.

The Bottom Line

I'm no energy-policy specialist. And it's entirely possible that Enron was right on some of the issues it asked the government to endorse and, thus, the Bush-Cheney task force might have been actually serving the public interest even as it agreed with Enron. But it simply cannot be possible that, on all 17 issues, Enron was on the side of the angels.

It's especially stunning to see Bush and Cheney taking anti-states-rights positions, or prowind-power positions, none of which most analysts might have predicted from their overall political philosophies. Enron out-lobbied powerhouses like the Western Governors Association and the American Public Power Association, two groups with close ties to Bush. Very impressive.

Near as I can tell, the Bush-Cheney energy task force agreed with Enron on darn near everything. Why even bother with the fig leaf of a task force? Why not—in the spirit of Republican efficiency and privatization—just turn the whole shootin' match over to Enron?

Wait a minute. I was trying to be ironic, but irony becomes impossible when you're merely describing reality. Bush and Cheney did turn huge amounts of America's public policy over to Enron; a corporation that will go down in history as representing corruption, arrogance and venality.

From having its way with the Bush-Cheney energy task force to handpicking the regulators it wanted and bullying regulators it did not want, Enron was the dominant corporation in an administration dominated by big corporations. We may never know if George W. Bush really did lobby the Argentines for Kenny-Boy. So far as I can tell, he's never discussed the allegation; the pro-Bush press corps in campaign 2000 was too charmed by Bush's frat-boy sense of humor to raise such uncomfortable issues with him, and now that he's in the protective bubble of the White House, he damn sure ain't talking.

This we know: the improbable political career of George W. Bush and the corrupt history of Enron are joined at the hip. Or the wallet.

Mama always told me you could judge a fellow by the company he keeps.

EIGHT

Taking Care of Bidness: Bush and Harken Energy

"The SEC fully investigated the stock deal. I was exonerated."—George W. Bush, defending himself against charges of insider trading.[1]

This letter "must in no way be construed as indicating that the party (George W. Bush) has been exonerated. . . ."—Bruce A. Hiler, Associate Director for Enforcement, Securities and Exchange Commission, in a letter to Bush's attorney, dated October 18, 1993.[2]

"I'm all name and no money."—Oilman George W. Bush, in a 1986 interview.[3]

"We were buying political influence. That was it. He was not much of a businessman."—George Soros, who owned one-third of Harken Energy, on why Harken bought Bush's failed oil company in 1986.[4]

"In the corporate world, sometimes things aren't exactly black and white when it comes to accounting procedures."—President George W. Bush, trying to defend the accounting practices he used at Harken Energy. News conference, the White House (7/8/02).[5]

"The people at Enron could have gone to school on this thing."—Alfred King, former managing director of the Institute of Management Accountants, vice chairman of Milwaukee-based Valuation Research Corp. and former advisor to the Financial Accounting Standards Board, commenting on the actions of Harken Energy's Board of Directors when Bush served on it.[6]

"I think we've given you every explanation possible."—White House Press Secretary Ari Fleischer on Bush's late SEC filings.[7]

"There was no malfeance involved. This was an honest disagreement about accounting procedures. . . . There was no malfeance, no attempt to hide anything."—George W. Bush, News conference, the White House (7/8/02).[8]

"It's Forrest Gump does finance. Every time he seemed to be in trouble, he would end up with a box of chocolates."—Charles Lewis, Center for Public Integrity (7/20/02).[9]

ANYONE WHO READ MOLLY IVINS AND LOUIS DUBOSE'S EXCELLENT book, *Shrub*, or even got to page 32 of my book, *Is Our Children Learning?*, was not shocked by the revelations of insider deals, accounting manipulation and alleged insider trading by George W. Bush when he was in the oil business. The national press, however, seduced by Dubya's charm and annoyed by Gore's know-it-all attitude, virtually ignored Bush's sordid record as a businessman.

Until now.

Again, in an act of heroic restraint, I will resist saying "I told you so." But all of this was there for the pro-Bush corporate media elite back when the American people could have done something useful with the information—like help Al Gore win by even *more* than 500,000 votes.

Still, Bush's record at Harken is important today, and perhaps even more relevant today than in 2000, since Bush is now trying to lead us in a crusade against corporate irresponsibility. Of course,

George W. Bush trying to lead us in a fight against corporate abuse is like John Walker Lindh leading us into battle against the Taliban.

Just Another Small Bidnessman from Midland

Although he once said, "I understand small business growth. I was one,"[10] George Walker Bush was no ordinary small businessman in Midland, Texas in the 1970s and '80s. For one thing, he had an Ivy League education (undergraduate degree from Yale, MBA from Harvard), and a trust fund. He also had another asset—one that proved far more valuable than his elite diplomas: his daddy's name. As he once put it, "I'm all name and no money."[11] He started Arbusto Energy (*arbusto* is Spanish for "bush") and, as it was going down, he sold a 10 percent stake in the company to the CEO of a Panamanian-based firm for $1 million. Now, you'd think that if ten percent of Bush's company is worth a million dollars, then the whole shootin' match would be worth, oh, say, $10 million.

Wrong. The book value of the entire Bush oil company was $382,376. How did Dubya get $1 million for 10 percent of a company whose total value was less than $400,000? I'm telling you, the man's a genius. But, humble man that he is, all Dubya would say was, "A company balance sheet can be misleading."[12]

Our hero later abandoned any pretense of bilingual nuance by renaming his firm Bush Exploration. It failed. Bush Exploration was bought by an outfit called Spectrum 7. Soon, it, too, was on the rocks. Lest you think Dubya had the Midas touch in reverse, consider this: Whereas any other failed businessman would have, well, failed, somehow Dubya always found a sugar daddy who was willing to overpay for a failed Bush business. Here again, Bush's business partners are too modest to boast about W's business acumen. William O. DeWitt, Jr., one of the men who ran Spectrum 7, said Bush was not exactly making the gut-wrenching decisions of running the company: "I can't remember any."[13]

So, Spectrum 7 was bought by Harken Energy in 1986. This is where it gets real interesting. At the time, billionaire investor George Soros owned one-third of Harken. He was asked years later why such an astute businessman would buy a collapsing Midland oil company, and he said, "We were buying political influence. That was it. He was not much of a businessman."[14]

Diogenes can put down his lantern. We've found an honest billionaire businessman.

E. Stuart Watson, who served on Harken's board with Bush,
seems to back up Soros's conclusion. "We didn't have a fair price for
oil, but we had George," he said.[15]

Aloha Also Means Rip-off

As a director of Harken Energy, Bush approved of a transaction that
is still controversial today: the sale of a Harken subsidiary to Harken
insiders.[16] Harken was up a creek without a paddle—it was losing
money fast. So the board, including Bush, agreed to sell off one of
Harken's assets: a chain of gas stations in Hawaii called Aloha Petroleum.

The "buyers" "paid" about $12 million for Aloha, which would
allow Harken to record an $8 million profit on the deal, greatly en-
hancing its puny bottom line.[17] I didn't put the words "buyers" and
"paid" in quotation marks to make some ironic, "air quotes" kind
of gesture (okay, I did just then, but not in the previous sentence). I
did it because the whole thing wasn't quite what it was cracked up to
be. The "buyers" were Harken insiders. The $12 million "sale" was
really just $1 million and an $11 million note—backed by Harken
itself.

It should be stressed that Bush himself was *not* one of the insiders
who "bought" Aloha, but he *was* one of the directors who approved
the deal.[18] Then again, so did Harken's accountants (you guessed it):
Arthur Andersen. The *Los Angeles Times* exhaustively analyzed the
deal, and concluded: "Based on a review of publicly released Securities and Exchange Commission filings, meeting minutes, memos and
correspondence from that period, there is no evidence that Bush, or
any of the other directors, raised objections or expressed concern
about the Aloha deal. Experts on corporate governance say that as an
independent director and one of only three members of the audit
committee, Bush was in a position to exercise an important oversight
role but apparently failed to do so."[19]

So, Harken's annual report for 1989 showed a profit of $8 million
on the sale of Aloha Petroleum. This little trick allowed Harken to
lead investors to believe the sale of Aloha had actually brought in an
$8 million profit, when in truth it had yielded little more than $1 mil-

lion and a bunch of IOUs—IOUs backed by a note from the company itself, so they'd be more accurately described as IO-Me's.

Smelling a rat, the Securities and Exchange Commission forced Harken to restate its losses. Harken was forced to amend its 1989 annual report. The January 31, 1991 amended filing declared that Harken's 1989 losses were actually 400 percent higher than they'd reported—an eye-popping $12,566,000, rather than the $3,300,000 loss it had declared earlier.[20] The SEC could have gone further, and charged Harken with fraud, but it chose not to.

Still, the insider sale of Aloha, which was approved by Bush, has not exactly received the stamp of approval from experts in accounting and ethics. "The people at Enron could have gone to school on this thing," said Alfred King, former managing director of the Institute of Management Accountants, vice chairman of Milwaukee-based Valuation Research Corp. and former advisor to the Financial Accounting Standards Board.

"They sold to themselves and recorded a profit," King said. "That's exactly what Enron did on a number of those off-balance-sheet transactions. On this one transaction at least, it's almost identical."[21]

Bush doesn't see the comparison. Indeed, the man who prides himself on his black-and-white, good-versus-evil, unnuanced world view sounded a lot like a moral relativist when he was asked about the Aloha deal. "In the corporate world, sometimes things aren't exactly black and white when it comes to accounting procedures."[22]

And the man who loves to give sanctimonious sermons about all manner of conduct suddenly clammed up when Mike Allen of the *Washington Post* asked him about his role in the Aloha deal. "Mike," Bush snapped, "You need to look back on the directors' minutes."[23]

Trouble is, Allen *couldn't* "look back on the directors' minutes" as Bush had recommended. The White House refused to provide them. White House Communications Director Dan Bartlett told reporters, "These are company documents. I can't release something I don't have." According to the *Washington Post*, "Harken has declined to release board records ever since questions about Bush's record on the board were raised during his first campaign for Texas governor, in 1994."[24]

Sure doesn't look like Bush is very proud of his service on the Harken board in general, and his role in approving the Aloha insider sale in particular.

"Hiding losses in partnerships, playing games with accounting, not reporting forthrightly transactions as a potential inside trader—it's all eerily reminiscent of Enron," Charles Lewis, of the nonpartisan Center for Public Integrity, told the *LA Times*. "This is not a corporate executive who laid awake at night worrying about complying with federal laws, from all appearances."[25]

When Is a Loan Not a Loan?

As a Harken insider, Bush was able to borrow a total of $180,375 from the struggling company. The loans were given at a 5 percent interest rate (in 1989, when he got the loans, the prime rate was 10.87 percent.[26]) Even better, Bush's loans were what's called *nonrecourse notes*, which carry no liability to the borrower in the event of default.[27] Basically, the deal was this: Bush borrowed money from Harken to buy stock in Harken. If the stock went up, Bush could sell, repay the loan and pocket the profit. But, if the stock went down, Bush could walk away and never repay the loan. And indeed, Bush never did repay the loan. The Harken board voted to "forgive" the loan in 1990.[28] I've always liked Alexander Pope's saying "To err really is human, to forgive divine." But forgiving $180,375? When the company is sinking in red ink?

Nothing divine about that.

You want to see a banker laugh his ass off? Go into the bank nearest you and ask for that deal.

A Man of His Most Recent Word

On April 4, 1990, Harken board member George W. Bush signed what's known as a *lockup* letter. In it, Bush pledged not to sell any stock for at least six months after the effective date of a proposed public stock offering.[29]

Now, everyone knows George W. Bush is a man of his word. A man who—as he said *ad nauseam* in the campaign of 2000—"knows what the meaning of 'is' is." He's the straight shooter, the plain-spoken, straight-talking Texan.

Wanna bet?

Just two months after pledging—in writing—not to sell any Harken stock, with Harken facing a sudden financial crisis, Dubya sold some stock. Well, that's not exactly true. He didn't just sell *some*. He sold two-thirds of all the Harken stock he held: nearly $850,000 worth of stock.[30]

Bush gave his word, and he broke his word. To put it charitably, I guess you could say he's a man of his most recent word.

This matters for reasons that go beyond Bush's honor. You see, Dubya has always claimed that he sold his Harken stock *not* because the stock was about to tank due to bad financial news (news that as a member of the firm's board of directors and audit committee you'd think Bush might know; news that had not yet been reported to the public). He sold, he claims, only because he needed to pay off a bank loan he'd taken out to buy a share of the Texas Rangers baseball team. The Associated Press reported that his story didn't ring true to independent attorneys and accountants they interviewed. Christopher Bebel, a Houston securities lawyer, told the AP that the fact that Bush had extra cash left over from the Harken sale even though he'd already paid off the loan for the Rangers purchase, as well as taxes, suggests "the possibility that Bush's liabilities did not prompt him to sell the Harken stock." Even if Bush had a preexisting plan to pay off his debts, as his attorneys told the SEC in the insider trading probe, "Bush still could have met his obligations by selling only a small portion of his Harken Energy stock," said Bebel.[31]

Almost Haven: Bush's Tax Dodge to the Caymans

"Taxes," Oliver Wendell Holmes famously wrote, "are what we pay for a civilized society." George W. Bush seems to have a different view. At Harken Energy, his attitude was "Taxes are paid by suckers."

Astonishing though it may be to you, this great patriot, this man who enjoys nothing more than waving the flag, served on the board of a company that behaved like a corporate Benedict Arnold, setting up an overseas subsidiary in order to avoid paying its fair share of taxes.

As president, Bush has criticized corporations that set up such sham subsidiaries to avoid taxes. He had his press secretary condemn the practice, telling the New York *Daily News*, "The President is concerned about corporations in America who take advantage, set up operations outside of America, in an effort to lower their taxes."[32]

Then, the *Daily News* lowered the boom, revealing that, in 1989, with Bush on the board of directors, Harken set up a subsidiary in the Cayman Islands, one of the most popular tax havens. When confronted about this massive hypocrisy, this decidedly unpatriotic act, Bush said, "I think we ought to look at people who are trying to avoid U.S. taxes as a problem," he said. "I think American companies ought to pay taxes here, and be good citizens."[33]

If Bush truly wants "to look at people who are trying to avoid U.S. taxes," he ought to get a mirror.

His flunkies and flaks were even more brazen. White House press secretary Ari Fleischer actually called the sleazy deal "a project in the Cayman Islands."[34]

A project? Ari, buddy, washing the car is a project. Mowing the lawn—that's a project. Cleaning out the garage—project. Setting up a sham subsidiary in the Cayman Islands to avoid paying the taxes you owe to the government that protects you, the soldiers that defend you, the nation that sustains you—that's economic treason.

Fleischer went on to spin the press that the subsidiary was not set up to avoid taxes. Right, Ari. And your hair looks *perfect*. No, really, the spokesfibber said, Harken wasn't trying to avoid taxes—just liability from an explosion or some other catastrophe as they drilled for oil in Bahrain.[35]

So, here's the Bush defense: I wasn't trying to evade the *taxes* of the United States, just the *laws* of the United States. Whatever happened to Bush's fabled call for Americans to take more personal responsibility? Wouldn't evading the liability laws be, well, trying to evade responsibility for something you're liable for?

Moreover, as the *Wall Street Journal* noted, "tax experts say such arrangements—while having liability implications—also typically have favorable tax consequences, since they let companies defer paying their U.S. taxes so long as profits are kept overseas."[36]

Finally, Fleischer and the fabricators said, the deal didn't provide any tax advantages because the income it was established to shield— from drilling offshore of the Persian Gulf state of Bahrain—never materialized because Bush and company couldn't find any oil. This is like saying that when I stuck the gun in the old lady's face and threatened her life, she died of a heart attack, so I didn't have to use the gun. Therefore, I'm not a murderer. (By the way, tiny, struggling Harken beat out Amoco for the Bahrain drilling contract. Could that have had anything to do with the fact that Poppy was in the White House at the time? Naaaah. Oil-rich Persian Gulf emirates frequently give drilling contracts to struggling oil companies that have never drilled offshore before. Sure. You bet.)

When he was questioned by reporters, Bush tried to look like he had nothing to hide. He even promised them that he'd help them get to the bottom of his slimy business dealings at Harken, saying, "As far as the Harken issue, we'll try to answer all your questions on that."

But he didn't. He continued to refuse to release all the records of his investigation by the SEC. He continued to refuse to call on Harken Energy to release the minutes of its board meetings and other documents that could allow the press and the public to know the full story of Bush's corporate conduct. It was a classic bait and switch.

Senate Majority Leader Tom Daschle of South Dakota said it best. He shook his head and remarked, "It gets harder and harder to take his position on corporate accountability seriously."

Bush's Alleged Insider Trading

This aspect of Bush's corporate conduct has probably gotten more ink than the others; when you pull it all together it really *is* a remarkable story.

First, for those of you who are not burdened with a legal education, here's a primer on the law of insider trading: Insider trading generally means buying or selling a security while in possession of material, nonpublic information about that security. It is a crime because corporate insiders possess information the general public does not. The bargain between buyer and seller is not equal—and, more important, cannot be equal—because one party has important information about the company that the other does not.

To commit insider trading, you need to either be an insider, or be someone who was tipped off by an insider. The Securities and Exchange Commission offers this illustration: "Corporate officers, directors, and employees who traded the corporation's securities after learning of significant, confidential corporate developments" are guilty of insider trading.[37] Insider trading undermines investors' faith in capital markets since, if insiders are buying and selling stock based on information they have and you can't get, investing in stocks becomes a fool's game for anyone who's not an insider. "Because insider trading undermines investor confidence in the fairness and integrity of the securities markets," the SEC says, "the Commission has treated the detection and prosecution of insider trading violations as one of its enforcement priorities."[38]

We shall soon see about that.

Bush was a member of Harken Energy Corporation's board of directors and of its audit, fairness and special committees.[39] He was also a consultant to the company.[40] Looks like an insider to me. There's nothing wrong with being an insider per se.

And he clearly traded. On June 22, 1990, Bush sold 212,140 shares of Harken stock, which was valued at $4 per share. Here again, not necessarily anything wrong with selling stock (unless you promised not to, but we already know all about that).

Here's where it gets dicey. Just two months after Bush sold, Harken announced its losses for the June 30, 1990 quarter. The value of Harken's stock fell to $2.37 per share immediately following the announcement of losses and was trading at only $1 by the end of the year.[41]

Bush adamantly denies that he knew about Harken's deteriorating financial situation when he sold. "I absolutely had no idea and would not have sold had I known," he told the *Dallas Morning News* in 1994.[42]

I want to believe Dubya on this. Really, I do. After all, I wasn't there. How can I know what Bush knew and when Bush knew it? (And, besides, any time George W. Bush pleads ignorance, he's got some credibility with me.)

However, there are some big holes in Bush's story. The first one was caused by an old Bush buddy. E. Stuart Watson Harken served with Dubya on the Harken board, as well as on the audit committee. When he was asked in 1994 if he and Bush were well informed about Harken's deteriorating financial picture, he said, "You bet we were."[43] According to Mr. Watson, both he and Bush "were kept current on the company's finances and knew that losses were to be announced." Watson added that earnings reports at Harken "were never a surprise to us." As members of the audit committee, he and Bush were briefed by the company treasurer and the inside and outside auditors. Bush vigorously disputes Watson's version, insisting, "Stuart Watson's memory is not right."[44]

I don't know who to believe. I really don't. But, as one of my law school profs used to say, let's test the credibility of the witnesses by asking the simple question: Who has something to gain from lying? Stuart Watson was and is a friend and political supporter of George W. Bush. He has nothing to gain, and much to lose (not the least of which is his friendship with the president of the United States), by asserting that he and Bush were fully aware of Harken's financial setbacks. George W. Bush, on the other hand, has everything to gain by asserting that he didn't know about the financial mess.

You decide who to believe. Before you do, consider that, according to the Associated Press, "As a Harken director, he [Bush] received memos in spring 1990 that referred in stark terms to the company's cash-strapped condition as banks demanded it pay down its debts. One document said the company was in the midst of a 'liquidity crisis' and another told Bush the company was 'in a state of noncompliance' with its lenders."[45]

Internal Harken Energy documents noted that the company's immediate cash needs [were] at a crisis "survivor" level in May 1990— just weeks before Bush dumped 212,000 shares of Harken stock. An internal Harken Energy Corporation "Analysis of Cash Needs" dated May 4, 1990 and covering May 1–July 31, indicated that Harken needed a cash infusion of $30 million to "maintain survivor status, pay past due payables of $2 million and rebuild working capital of $3 million." In order to maintain "minimum operations," the company needed a "cash infusion of $38 million . . . to maintain minimum operational flexibility."[46]

From the records we have, it sure looks like Harken was in deep doo-doo (as Poppy would say) and that Dubya knew about it when he sold. Poor Junior. He really is in a tough position. Either he knew the company was on the skids when he broke his promise and sold out, in which case he was dancing on the edge of insider trading—or he had no idea that the company's finances were going south, which means he wasn't much of a businessman, consultant, board member and audit committee member.

The Dog Ate My SEC Disclosure

Regardless of whether or not he knew of Harken's financial problems, Bush had another problem: a legal one. As an insider, he was obligated to report to the Securities and Exchange Commission that he had sold stock in Harken. He didn't do it—not until more than four months later.

And that wasn't the only time. Not by a long shot. Failing to disclose relevant information in a timely manner is a recurrent problem with Dubya (and, no, I'm not just referring to his fib about not being arrested when in truth he'd been busted for drunk driving). In an April 9, 1991 memorandum, the Securities and Exchange Commission noted that Bush repeatedly failed to report stock transactions in a timely fashion. According to the SEC, "With respect to Harken, Bush has filed a timely Form 3 and four late Forms 4 reporting four separate transactions totaling $1,028,935. Bush's Forms 4 were filed from 15 to 34 weeks late." A 1991 form arrived approximately 34 weeks late. In 1987 he was about 17 weeks late reporting his acquisition of 212,152 shares of Harken stock. Also in 1987 he was 15 weeks late in reporting the exercise of options for $96,000. And in 1989 he was 15 weeks late in reporting another $84,375 worth of options.[47]

Disclosure of stock trades by corporate insiders is vital. It gives regular investors a window into the thinking of the people who know the most about the company. If the people in the know are buying, some investors might take that as a sign they should buy as well. And vice versa on selling. Disclosing insider transactions in a timely fashion is more than just a mundane, arcane matter of bureaucratic paperwork. It's an important part of maintaining honest financial markets.

Excuses, Excuses

Yogi Berra once said, "You can observe a lot by watching." Lately, I've been wondering what the people who have been on the receiving end of a Bush lecture about personal responsibility think when they watch Dubya weasel and waffle and bob and weave and blame and deny. Here is a brief compendium of the often hilarious and always self-serving excuses he's offered over the years for his failure to properly disclose his insider stock sales:

- **"I'm absolutely convinced I filed it."** When he was asked about it during his first campaign for governor, in 1994, Bush told reporters, "I'm absolutely convinced we filed every form necessary." [48]

- **"I'm pretty much certain that I filed it."** Bush to the *Houston Chronicle*, also in 1994. [49]

- **"The SEC lost it."** According to a 1994 article in the *Austin American-Statesman*, "Bush said his attorneys made the required filing, but the Securities and Exchange Commission lost it." An SEC spokesman could not back Bush up. "As far as I know," the spokesman said, "nobody ever found the 'lost' filing." [50]

- **"My lawyers lost it."** In a press briefing on July 3, 2002, White House Press Secretary Ari Fleischer told reporters, "The president thought it had been filed at the time, and indicated so publicly. What happened as a result was, it was a mixup with the attorneys dealing with the Form 4, and it was filed later."

- **"Uhhhh . . . I dunno."** Bush told reporters on July 8, 2002, "As to why the Form 4 was filed late, I still haven't figured it out completely." [51]

- **"I think we've given you every explanation possible."**— White House Press Secretary Ari Fleischer on why George W. Bush was late disclosing his insider stock sales. [52] No kidding, Ari.

"Fully Vetted" by the SEC?

When he is confronted with the proof of his behavior as a corporate director, Bush invariably retreats to one argument: that the SEC investigated this thoroughly and cleared him. Trouble is, neither of those claims are true. The SEC did *not* investigate Bush's conduct at Harken thoroughly, nor did the commission clear him. In fact, contrary to Bush's repeated assertions that his stock sale has been "fully investigated by the SEC," Bush was never even questioned by SEC investigators.[53] Nor, according to Bush's lawyer, Robert W. Jordan (now Bush's ambassador to Saudi Arabia), did the SEC talk to Harken CEO Mikel Faulkner. Nor did the commission talk to any other officer of the company. Nor was any other director questioned.[54]

Does that sound like a thorough investigation to you?

Of course, at the time of the investigation, Junior's daddy *was* president. The chairman of the Securities and Exchange Commission who investigated Dubya was Richard C. Breeden, a well-regarded man who had long-standing connections to the Bush family. Breeden's ties to the Bush family go at least as far back as George H. W. Bush's 1980 presidential campaign, for which Breeden performed get-out-the-vote work. Breeden served as a Bush adviser throughout the 1980s and served as then-Vice President Bush's deputy counsel. Breeden also served as Bush's point man on the 1989 savings and loan scandal, where he helped to shape the Bush administration's response to the crisis, before becoming Bush's choice to head the SEC.[55]

As SEC chairman, Breeden had an "unusually close" relationship with President Bush, according to the *Financial Times*. *USA Today* noted: "As for Breeden's unquestioned devotion to George Bush— huge color photographs of the president and other presidential memorabilia in his office overwhelm family photos—he makes no apology."[56]

During Breeden's tenure at the SEC, he gained the reputation of pushing decisions that helped to promote then-President Bush's agenda of the day and, more broadly, for "worshiping" Bush. According to *USA Today:* "He [Breeden] has a reputation for worshiping Bush, dropping everything to talk to a congressman, freezing out colleagues at the SEC and refusing to delegate work."[57]

Breeden's close ties to, and adoration of, Bush Senior is troubling enough to the credibility of the commission's inquiry into the boss's son. What compounds the concern is that the SEC's general counsel at the time was James R. Doty. Junior was no stranger to Doty. Doty in fact was a partner at the prestigious Texas law firm of Baker &

Botts, where he worked on the 1989 purchase of the Texas Rangers baseball team—one of whose purchasers was none other than George W. Bush.[58]

In an interview with the *Washington Post* this year, Doty said that he recused himself from the SEC's investigation of his former client George W. Bush's stock sale.[59] Good for him. But back in 1994, during Bush's first gubernatorial run in Texas, Doty claimed he didn't even know of an SEC investigation of Bush until after he left the SEC. Doty said that he had included Bush on a list of his legal clients that he gave to the SEC's solicitor, with instructions to keep him in the dark about any investigations involving former clients.[60] It's a pretty neat trick to recuse yourself from a case you knew nothing about. If Mr. Doty says he did, I'm willing to give him the benefit of the doubt. *If* they release all the records and the records prove him right.

Still, even giving Mr. Doty every benefit of the doubt, it's kind of hard to imagine that he didn't know about the Bush investigation. Leading up to the SEC's investigation of Bush's stock sale, almost every major print source in the country published reports of the transaction, such as the Associated Press (3/7/92), the *Dallas Morning News* (3/8/92), *U.S. News & World Report* (3/16/92); the *Wall Street Journal* (4/4/91), and *USA Today* (4/8/91).

It may be that Mr. Doty's not big on reading the papers. If, in fact, Mr. Doty recused himself, that's admirable. We'd know for sure if Bush would simply release all the records of the SEC's investigation. If it was so clean, if it was so thorough, and if he was cleared, he should be proud of the record, and want everyone to see it for themselves.

Disclosure, Disclosure, Disclosure

If the first three rules of real estate are "location, location, location," the first three rules of a public official under scrutiny are "disclosure, disclosure, disclosure." Bill and Hillary Clinton's privacy concerns about disclosing ancient records of a long-ago land deal in which they lost money led the media, the Republicans and too many Democrats, to call for an independent counsel. And the result was Ken Starr peeping into everybody's windows and pawing through everybody's underwear drawers.

Nobody wants that for Dubya. I'm not being sarcastic or ironic here. I have no desire to see Bush's personal life probed the way Clinton's was. But I do believe the American people have a right to know whether their president violated securities laws. Harvey Pitt, the head of the Securities and Exchange Commission, said that if Bush asked him to, he would release the SEC documents on whether Bush conducted insider trading.[61] Bush shouldn't just *ask* Pitt to release all the records, he should *order* him to do so.

There's only one way for Bush to reclaim his good name in the face of a mountain of evidence that he was up to his neck in some pretty serious corporate shenanigans—let it all out. The fact that he's stonewalling is strong evidence that he's got something to hide.

The Bottom Line

We'll never know the real bottom line on Bush's behavior while at Harken until all the records and facts come out. But those facts exist and, as the Scottish novelist and surgeon Tobias Smollet said, "facts are stubborn things."

We do know this: Even Bush's daddy's SEC refused to exonerate him. Every time you hear Junior say he was investigated and cleared by the SEC, keep in mind the letter the SEC sent him in 1993—a letter he requested because he was going to run for governor and wanted to wave around some sort of proof he'd been cleared. However, the SEC made a particular point of refusing to pronounce Dubya innocent. The decision not to charge Bush, the SEC wrote, "must in no way be construed as indicating that [Bush] has been exonerated."[62]

It would have been preferable if the campaign press corps had thoroughly covered the Harken issue before the election. For whatever reasons—journalistic, cultural or political—they did not. Now, with a crisis of confidence in the markets, with corporate wrongdoing rattling investors, a nation turns its lonely eyes to—Dubya? We ought to at least know whether the man who pledged to "restore honor and integrity to the Oval Office" conducted himself with honor and integrity in his business dealings.

NINE

Halliburton:
How Dick Cheney Put the
"Vice" in Vice President

"I get good advice, if you will, from their people based upon how we're doing business and how we're operating—over and above just sort of the normal by-the-books auditing arrangement."—Dick Cheney, appearing in a promotional video for Arthur Andersen.[1]

"Vice President Richard B. Cheney has had a distinguished career as a businessman . . ."—Official biography of the vice president of the United States. http://www.whitehouse.gov/vicepresident/vpbio.html

"I'm very proud of what I did at Halliburton . . . and I frankly don't feel any need to apologize for the way I've spent my time over the last five years as the CEO and chairman of a major American corporation."—Then–vice presidential candidate Richard B. Cheney.[2]

"With financial markets reeling from the wave of corporate scandals, the vice president's past as a corporate chieftain has become a liability. . . . The Securities and Exchange Commission is investigating Halliburton to see if the company used misleading accounting tricks to inflate its profits."—ABC News (7/19/02).

"If you're a CEO and you think you can fudge the books in order to make yourself look better, we're going to find you, we're going to arrest you, and we're going to hold you to account"—George W. Bush, 7/29/02, *Washington Post*, (7/30/02).

"Duty, Honor, Unwavering Leadership"

Those are the words that Dick Cheney uses to describe . . . Dick Cheney. Seriously. (Of course, everything Dick Cheney does he takes seriously.) If you want to see an exercise in self-adoration that would make Narcissus blush, check out Vice President Cheney's official biography on the White House website, www.whitehouse.gov. In his official bio, Cheney (or his staff) tells us he "served with duty, honor, and unwavering leadership, gaining him the respect of the American people during trying military times."[3] Cheney goes on to tell us that "during his tenure in the House, [he] earned a reputation as a man of knowledge, character and accessibility."

Ralph Waldo Emerson once wrote of another man who loved to tell the world about his virtue: "The louder he talked of his honor, the faster we counted our spoons."[4] So, what is it about Dick Cheney that compels him and those around him to tell us over and over again what a man of character and honor and integrity he is, what a patriot he is? I don't know Dick Cheney and I'm perfectly open to the notion that he is all those things and more. The public record of the man's performance as CEO of Halliburton, however, conjures up a different vocabulary.

Fuzzy Math

Dick Cheney was the CEO of the Halliburton Company, an oil-services and construction giant, from 1995 to 2000. In the middle of Cheney's tenure—in 1998—Halliburton altered its accounting practices in a way some have found questionable, and that significantly affected Halliburton's bottom line. Halliburton did not notify investors of this change for more than a year.

The accounting change allowed Halliburton to book revenue on the assumption that its customers would pay disputed cost overruns on projects, rather than waiting for the customer to actually pay for the cost overruns before reporting the revenue. Thus, Halliburton was able to count disputed, potential revenue as if it were cash on hand. Arthur Andersen, the disgraced accounting firm that was convicted of impeding a federal investigation into the Enron collapse, approved the accounting change.

This is not a minor issue. According to the firm's financial reports, the cost overruns that Halliburton was counting as revenue represented half the company's operating profit in the fourth quarter of 1998.[5]

One way in which to grasp just how important this accounting change was is to look at how Halliburton fared in comparison to its competitors. In the quarter that it made the accounting change, according to Halliburton's SEC filings, its *accounts receivable*—sales that had been booked without the company having yet received payment—soared in comparison to Halliburton's competitors. According to the *New York Times*, "When Mr. Cheney became Halliburton's chief executive in October 1995, Halliburton had roughly 95 cents in receivables for every dollar in quarterly revenues. When he left in July 2000, the ratio was $1.20 in receivables for each dollar in quarterly sales. Over the same period, the average ratio of receivables to sales at five big competitors of Halliburton fell slightly, from 92 cents per dollar of sales in 1995 to 86 cents per dollar 5 years later." Pennsylvania State University accounting professor Edward Ketz said that the rapid rise in accounts receivable would have raised "a little bit of a red flag" to the company's executives that the accounting procedure was abnormal.[6]

Why would Halliburton monkey around with its accounting? The bottom line, baby. And Dick Cheney is a bottom-line kind of guy. New York University's Stern School of Business accounting department chairman Paul Brown said that Halliburton's accounting change was "clearly a way of pumping up revenues and receivables." Brown inquired how Halliburton could claim a customer had paid when that customer still had the right to dispute the charge. "There's already a conflict here, or there wouldn't be these claims," Brown said. "How did Halliburton estimate the possibility that the change order was going to be resolved?"[7]

The *New York Times* put it more directly: "At the time of the change—which was approved by Arthur Andersen, the company's auditors at the time—Halliburton was suffering big losses on some of its long-term contracts, according to filings. Its stock had slumped because of a recession in the oil industry. Two former executives of Dresser Industries, which merged with Halliburton in 1998, said that they concluded after the merger that Halliburton had instituted aggressive accounting practices to obscure its losses."[8]

In May 2002, the Securities and Exchange Commission began an investigation into whether the altered accounting practices by Halliburton were legal. According to a press release from Halliburton, the company "received notification from the Securities and Exchange Commission that it has initiated a preliminary investigation of the Company's accounting treatment of cost overruns on construction jobs."[9]

Cheney Praises Andersen for Going "Over and Above" Normal Arrangement

Cheney defenders say that, as CEO, Cheney was not responsible for internal operations, and therefore may not have been aware of the allegedly misleading accounting. The record suggests otherwise. Cheney was so impressed with Arthur Andersen, the accounting firm that approved the change, that he even appeared in a promotional video for Arthur Andersen to praise the auditing firm for the advice it gave him while he was Halliburton's CEO. "I get good advice, if you will, from their people based upon how we're doing business and how we're operating—over and above just sort of the normal by-the-books auditing arrangement," Cheney said on the tape. Andersen used the tape after Cheney became vice president and hyped his appearance in the tape by referring to him as "Vice President Dick Cheney, formerly of Halliburton" in the video and in marketing materials.[10]

I've read that statement over and over again. I've watched that piece of videotape again and again, and I keep reaching one inescapable conclusion: Dick Cheney was pleased that Arthur Andersen didn't follow the normal auditing arrangement. He says so, just as plain as day. And let us not forget that this is Dick Cheney speaking. This is a man from the West, a straight shooter who tells it like it is. A man who says what he means and means what he says.

So, when Dick Cheney says he was pleased that Arthur Andersen went "over and above just sort of the normal by-the-books auditing arrangement," I think we ought to take him at his word. Andersen did not go by the books when it audited Cheney's company, and Cheney was happy about it.

What Did Dick Know and When Did He Know It?

I was a liberal arts major. Although I was also educated as a lawyer, I don't have the technical expertise to know whether what Halliburton did with its books was fraudulent or perfectly acceptable or somewhere in between. I do know this: Dick Cheney was responsible for what went on at that company. Either he knew about these changes, or he should have known. Either way, he's responsible.

The current CEO of Halliburton—who was number two to Cheney in the '90s—says uncategorically that Cheney knew about the controversial accounting change. David Lesar told *Newsweek* that Cheney was aware that Halliburton counted cost overruns as revenue. "The Vice President was aware of who owed us money, and he helped us collect it," he said.[11]

People who saw Cheney in action during that period boasted of his hands-on style and his deep knowledge of the company. Byron Dunn, an oil analyst for UBS Warburg, told *USA Today* in the 2000 campaign he had seen Cheney "talk for three hours without notes" about the intricacies of Halliburton's business. "A common theme among executives who have seen Cheney in action," the paper reported, "is that he thrives on complexity."[12] Sounds like this accounting change was right up Cheney's alley.

Dick Cheney was the CEO. As such, he signed the company's financial statements—the allegedly misleading ones—in 1998 and 1999.[13] He hauled in $45 million in just five years.[14] His bio boasts of his "distinguished career as a businessman."[15] According to Halliburton's 1999 proxy statement, CEOs are evaluated by the board of directors on "leadership and vision; integrity; . . . performance of the business (including such measurements as total shareholder return and achievement of financial objectives and goals); development and implementation of initiatives to provide long-term economic benefit to the Company; accomplishment of strategic objectives and development of management."[16]

Cheney served as Halliburton's chairman of the board—as well as CEO—from January 1996 until September 1998. In that capacity, he was ultimately responsible for financial reporting. In its 1998 SEC 10-K form, Halliburton stated, "The Board, operating through its Audit Committee . . . provides oversight to the financial reporting process."[17] Dick Cheney was the chairman of the board. The buck stopped with him.

If the current Halliburton CEO is wrong when he says Cheney knew about the controversial accounting change—if, somehow, the CEO famous for immersing himself in the details of his company didn't know about this enormously consequential accounting matter—then he darn sure should have known. Lynn Turner is the former chief accountant at the Securities and Exchange Commission, and is now a professor of accounting at Colorado State University. In May 2002, she told the *New York Times* that the accounting changes that Halliburton undertook should have set off alarm bells: "If they changed their accounting from recording claims when they were settled and collected to recording claims at an earlier point in time, then that would raise a red flag and would raise a question as to whether it's a permissible change," Turner said.

Bush Says Cheney's Responsible and Should Pay (Sort Of)

In his Ten-Point Plan for corporate responsibility reform, President Bush states, "The CEO bears particular responsibility for informing the firm's shareholders of its financial health. This obligation goes well beyond complying with 'check-the-box' accounting. The CEO must be held responsible for informing investors about the financial condition of the public company and the risks it faces."[18]

Worse (for Cheney), proposal number four of Bush's Ten-Point Plan reads: "Under this proposal, CEO bonuses and other incentive-based forms of compensation would be disgorged in cases of accounting restatements resulting from misconduct."[19]

This is very bad news for Vice President Cheney because, during his tenure as CEO of Halliburton, Dick Cheney was awarded $5,861,102 in bonuses. From the point when Halliburton changed accounting procedures in 1998, Cheney earned $2,606,102 in bonuses.[20] So, if Bush's plan were law, and there was a ruling that Halliburton's accounting change was inappropriate, ol' Dick would be out more than two-and-a-half million bucks.

That's not all. Proposal number five of Bush's Ten-Point Plan states, "CEOs or other officers who clearly abuse their power should lose their right to serve in any corporate leadership positions. This proposal, which would require legislation, would authorize the SEC to ban individuals from serving as officers or directors of publicly held corporations if they engage in serious misconduct."[21]

I wonder if Bush's ban on serving as a corporate leader also applies to serving as a world leader? If so, then Cheney would not only be out $2.6 million, he'd also be out of a job. No more vice presidential mansion, no more secure, undisclosed location, no more getting his . . . well . . . ring kissed by the Washington press corps.

No wonder Cheney snarls all the time.

Come Clean, Dick

When Bill and Hillary Clinton's twenty-year-old failed land deal was in the papers, the calls for complete disclosure and full investigations and independent counsels and congressional hearings were deafening. Of course, Cheney and Halliburton is nothing like Whitewater. Whitewater was a small land deal that never took off, and in which the Clintons lost money. Halliburton is a multibillion-dollar corporation whose stock may have been inflated and has certainly fallen lately, costing perhaps thousands of investors millions of dollars. Yet there have been no hearings on Halliburton, no calls for independent counsels. Where are all the pious pontificators of the Republican establishment, who so boldly called for investigating the Clintons? They're busy using Dick Cheney to raise special-interest money for them.

Cheney's strategy on Halliburton is to stonewall. He and his staff refuse to answer any questions about the company, Cheney's work there, or the ethics of what Cheney did or did not do. They cite the ongoing SEC investigation. Of course, President Bush has not been so circumspect. At a press conference with Polish President Kwasniewski, he expressed confidence that the SEC would find that Cheney did nothing wrong at Halliburton.[22]

Now, it could be that Bush has such confidence in the SEC clearing Cheney because, as a former CEO and an MBA himself, he has a detailed and nuanced knowledge of the intricacies of accounting. Or, it could be, as an intuitive judge of character, he's able to discern the radiant goodness in Dick Cheney—the same goodness Cheney no doubt sees when he looks in the mirror. Or, it could be—just might be—a message to the SEC employees investigating Cheney (all of whom work for Dubya): "Clear him, Dan-O." And Bush's faith in the SEC would be well placed. After all, the SEC refused to prosecute Dubya for insider trading when his Poppy was president; why would it go after Dick Cheney now that Junior is president?

Over at Halliburton, they're not so sure. See, they're holding the bag now that Cheney's off running the country. And my guess is they're not going to go gently into that good night. Perhaps that's why Halliburton spokeswoman Wendy Hall has said, "At some point, [Cheney] is going to have to address these [accounting] issues."[23]

Dick Got the Gold Mine, We Got the Shaft

While the SEC probe is the only potential criminal exposure Cheney faces, his tenure as CEO of Halliburton raises other interesting issues about how men like Bush and Cheney think the world ought to work. In just five years, Dick Cheney made $45 million at Halliburton—so much money that even his grandchildren need never work a day in their lives. Did Cheney's performance merit that sort of payoff? Cheney certainly thinks so. At a campaign stop in Oregon in 2000, Cheney bragged, "By any measure you want to use, Halliburton has been a great success story."[24]

Here's a measure: the stock price. If, in October 1995 when Dick Cheney took over Halliburton, you'd invested in the Standard & Poor's 500—a broad index of big companies—your stock would be worth 83 percent more in May 2002 (the most recent figures I had at this writing.) Not bad, given the volatility of the stock market. If you had, instead, invested in Dick Cheney's Halliburton, you would have *lost* 56 percent. The difference between making 83 percent and losing 56 percent is the difference between a well-run company and a poorly run one. The net result of Cheney's reign at Halliburton was a short-term jolt in the stock (at which point Cheney sold out, due to government ethics requirements), then a painful collapse, leaving investors and employees worse off.[25]

The corporate compensation expert Graef Crystal, put Cheney's tenure and performance into perspective—and was even a little generous. "He was," Crystal said, "sort of an average performer for his industry."[26]

Here's another measure: jobs. As CEO, Cheney laid off 10,100 workers.[27]

Or how 'bout benefits? Cheney, who has had some rather well-publicized medical problems of his own, cut health benefits for Halliburton retirees.[28]

All of us understand that companies sometimes go through tough times. Layoffs, and even benefit cuts, are sometimes a painful reality, necessary for the company to survive tough times and preserve the jobs and benefits of the rest of its employees. But Dick Cheney sucked $45 million out of Halliburton for himself. Forty-five million dollars—in just five years. While men and women who'd given their entire working lives to Halliburton were laid off, while retirees who had nowhere to turn had their health benefits cut. Nice, Dick. How many people had to come home to their families heartbroken, panic-stricken, with a knot in their stomach, too sad and ashamed to even tell their wife or husband that their job at Halliburton was over? How many retirees got a letter in the mail notifying them their health benefits were going to be cut—and how many of them, like Dick Cheney, had a bad ticker or cancer or gout (Cheney's had all three)? All of that pain for all of those people. And Dick Cheney walked away with $45 million. Either the company was doing so well its CEO deserved a vast fortune, in which case it shouldn't have been firing workers and cutting retirees' health benefits, or Halliburton was struggling, in which case its CEO certainly didn't deserve $45 million for mediocre performance.

How about treating employees fairly? In November 1997, Halliburton told its employees that if they continued to come to work it meant they agreed to surrender their right to sue Halliburton, and have arbitration as their only recourse. A 30-year veteran employee,

James Myers, subsequently sued Halliburton when he believed he was being discriminated against because of his race and age. Keep in mind, this is a 30-year veteran of the company, not some fly-by-night artist looking for a quick lawsuit. Tough luck, Mr. Myers. At Dick Cheney's Halliburton reporting for work means you check your rights at the door. Or, as the *Austin Chronicle* put it: "The screwed can't sue."[29]

One interesting footnote to that case: the all-Republican, all-right-wing Texas Supreme Court upheld Halliburton's right to screw its employees. One of the justices who voted for Halliburton and against the Texan who was suing was one Priscilla Owen. The same Priscilla Owen who was a Bush-Cheney nominee for the powerful Fifth Circuit Court of Appeals—one step below the U.S. Supreme Court.

Trading with the Enemy

Or how about patriotism, Dick? A measure you seem to like being judged by—as long as you're the one doing the judging. Like his boss, Dick Cheney has never fought in a war. He said he had "other priorities" in the '60s.[30] Now that he's beyond draft age, he's Super Patriot—in word, if not in deed. In fact, his deeds tell a very different story.

As CEO of Halliburton, Dick Cheney did business with some of the most brutal and ruthless enemies of freedom, including Saddam Hussein's Iraq, the ayatollahs' Iran, and Mu'ammar Qadhafi's Libya. North Korea is the only "axis of evil" nation that Cheney didn't try to make a buck off of.

Let's start with the worst: Iraq. How a man who served as Secretary of Defense during the last Gulf War could do business with Saddam Hussein is beyond me. In fact, it's beyond the law. It's illegal for U.S. companies to do business with Iraq (except for the UN-supervised oil-for-food program), but Halliburton got around the law by using foreign subsidiaries.

After being chosen as Bush's running mate in 2000, Cheney initially denied that Halliburton had any dealings in Iraq, saying he "had a firm policy that we wouldn't do anything in Iraq, even arrangements that were supposedly legal."[31] The trouble with that denial is that in 1998, CEO Cheney had overseen Halliburton's acquisition of Dresser Industries, a company that exported equipment to Iraq through two of its subsidiaries, Dresser Rand and Ingersoll Dresser Pump. A Halliburton spokesperson confirmed the two companies were joint ventures with Halliburton while Cheney was CEO.[32]

Cheney claimed that he didn't know these subsidiaries were dealing with the Iraqi regime when Halliburton took them over.[33]

Baloney.

James E. Perella, Ingersoll-Rand's former chairman, thinks Halliburton execs must have known about the links to Iraq: "They obviously did due diligence."[34]

Let's say, for the sake of argument, that I'm too distrusting of Cheney. Let's say that he didn't know about the sales to Iraq in September 1998 when Halliburton took over Dresser. What about after that? United Nations records show that under Cheney, the two companies continued signing lucrative contracts with Saddam's Iraq for more than a year.[35] According to the *Washington Post*, "Former executives at the subsidiaries said they had *never heard any objections—from Cheney or any other Halliburton official—to trading with Baghdad.*" (Emphasis added.)[36] The *Post* concluded that newly obtained UN documents revealed that "the dealings were more extensive than originally reported and than Vice President Cheney has acknowledged . . . Cheney has offered contradictory accounts of how much he knew about Halliburton's dealings with Iraq."[37]

That's putting it mildly. It's more accurate to say that Cheney has offered nothing but falsehoods, fibs and fabrications about his trading with the enemy.

Libya, O Libya

Halliburton used another subsidiary—this one British—to conduct business in Libya, evading a Reagan-imposed ban. According to David Lesar, who ran Halliburton's day-to-day operations under Cheney and is now Halliburton's CEO, when Cheney arrived at Halliburton, he told company executives he wanted to end Halliburton's Libyan operations. According to Lesar, Cheney changed his mind when he became convinced such a move would hurt Halliburton's relationship with its customers.[38]

What was that his bio said about "unwavering leadership"?

Tehran Is Lovely This Time of Year

Cheney's Halliburton was so brazen in terms of its operations in Iran that it even set up shop there. That's right. While Dick Cheney was CEO, his firm, using a subsidiary called Halliburton Products and Services, opened an office in beautiful downtown Tehran. When confronted about this massive hypocrisy, Cheney's spokesperson in the vice president's office, Juleanna Glover Weiss, refused to comment—except to say that "the vice president is no longer head of Halliburton and has severed all ties to the company."

Duh, Juleanna. Cheney left Halliburton when he became vice president of the United States. It's been in all the papers. That doesn't negate the fact that Halliburton opened an office in Tehran *while Cheney was running Halliburton.* Needless to say, Iran is another of Dubya's "axis of evil" nations, and has been identified by the U.S. State Department as a state sponsor of terrorism since 1993.[39]

In fact, Cheney wanted to do *more* business in Iran. Just weeks before Bush put him on the national ticket, in June 2000, Cheney called for an end to U.S. sanctions against Iran that prevent American companies from doing business there. Speaking at the World Petroleum Congress in Calgary, Alberta, Canada, Cheney said, "I would hope we could find ways to improve [U.S.–Iran relations]. One of the ways, I think, is to allow American firms to do the same thing that most other firms around the world are able to do now, and that is to be active in Iran. . . . We're kept out of there primarily by our own government, which has made a decision that U.S. firms should not be allowed to invest significantly in Iran, and I think that's a mistake."[40]

Cheney did more than give speeches about his desire to enrich and support and sustain the enemies of freedom and sponsors of terrorism in the Middle East, he used his status as a former defense secretary and former member of Congress to actively lobby for repealing sanctions against Iran and Libya. As CNN reported, "When U.S. trade sanctions kept Halliburton from doing business in Iran and other countries, Cheney began pressing his former colleagues in Congress to lift the sanctions." This despite the fact that Libya (like Iran) has been designated as a sponsor of terrorism by the State Department since 1993.[41]

Shortly after joining the GOP ticket, Cheney was challenged to defend his outrageous and unpatriotic actions as a businessman. ABC's Sam Donaldson went right after Cheney, saying, "With Halliburton you were very insistent that you wanted to do business with Iran. You wanted to do business with Libya. In fact, you said, 'We'd like to do more with Iran than we're able to do.'" Cheney responded, "When I was chairman and CEO of Halliburton, my responsibility and obligations are my shareholders, my employees, my customers. And—and I do have a firm belief that unilateral economic sanctions rarely work."[42]

There is a phrase that describes how something can be seen as acceptable in one context—say, when you're a money-grubbing businessman—but wrong in another—say, when you're a flag-waving politician. It's called *situational ethics.* Another name for it is *moral relativism*—the notion that there is no inherent right or wrong, it all depends on your perspective. So, here again, if you're only interested in making a buck, and there are bucks to be made from doing business with the lunatics who took Americans hostage in Tehran, or who blew up a Berlin disco full of soldiers and a plane full of innocents, as Qadhafi's Libya did, or who invaded Kuwait and waged war against America, as Saddam Hussein did—it's all okay. But where, oh where, were the morality mavens of the right when Cheney was descending into this morass? The same right-wing blowhards who pompously and piously lectured us about Clinton's relationship with Monica Lewinsky were strangely silent about Dick Cheney's relationship with Iran, Iraq and Libya.

Charles Lewis of the Center for Public Integrity does not suffer from moral relativism. "Cheney and Halliburton have done business in some of the nastiest countries on the earth," he said, "and whenever you are doing international commerce you are frequently confronted with all kinds of moral choices that some people would like to avoid. I think this does raise questions of improper influence."[43]

Cheney saw things differently. He once summed up his philosophy in a speech to Amarillo, Texas, oilmen: "You've got to go where the oil is," he said. "I don't worry about it a lot."[44] The "it" in this case was the potential for political instability in central Asia, but the overall philosophy seems to have carried Cheney into business with America's enemies.

"Bermuda, Bahama, Come On Pretty Mama . . ."

If Cheney's mantra began with "You've got to go where the oil is," it ended with "and you've got to hide your profits where the taxes ain't." As CEO of Halliburton he set up between 20 and 35 overseas tax havens.[45] And, to add insult to injury, Cheney's office, like Bush, denied the subsidiaries—all set up in tax havens—were intended to avoid U.S. taxes. Why else do you set up subsidiaries in the Cayman Islands, or Barbados or Bermuda? As Joe Conason suggested in Salon.com, "Maybe they just all like rum drinks and snorkeling."[46] In point of fact, the strategy worked. In two of the five years Cheney was CEO—1995 and 1999—Halliburton paid no federal income tax. None. Zip. Zilch. Nada.[47]

Duty, honor and unwavering leadership, indeed.

The Bottom Line

Dick Cheney's conduct as CEO of Halliburton is nothing less than scandalous. His number two at Halliburton says Cheney knew all about controversial accounting practices that are now under investigation. Under his leadership, Halliburton's stock jumped up, Cheney sold out (albeit to become vice president), little people got screwed, and the feds are investigating. If you trust Bush and Cheney's SEC to investigate Cheney, I've got some oceanfront property in Arizona I'd like to sell you (as George Strait once sang). Under Cheney, Halliburton traded with the most evil nations on earth, and sought to avoid taxes in the most decent, honorable and generous nation in the world, the United States of America. Richard B. Cheney is a poster boy for all that is wrong with the Bush Republican economic philosophy.

TEN

The Keystone Kops:
Bush and His Economic Team

"He [Bush] obviously has not been very effective. People knew when they listened to Clinton that there was something behind him. There was Bob Rubin, there was an economic team. I don't think the markets see anything behind this President's words."—Republican Senator Chuck Hagel, *New York Times* (8/12/02).

"This has been an underlying worry even before the crisis, that Bush did not have a strong economic team . . . There is a different emphasis in this White House than the last."—Kathleen Stephansen, Senior Economist, Credit Suisse First Boston, *Evening Standard* (10/1/01).

"There's a sense that the White House is providing almost no economic leadership."—Stephen Moore, president of the Club for Growth, which supports conservative candidates for Congress. *Washington Times* (10/22/01).

"Now is the moment Paul O'Neill, Pitt, Commerce Secretary Don Evans, White House economic aide Larry Lindsey, and Bush's other top moneymen need to prove that they aren't the Keystone Kops of federal finance. The economy, and

Bush's presidency, may depend on it. But so far they've failed."
Fortune (9/2/02).

"Companies come and go. Part of the genius of capitalism is
people get to make good decisions or bad decisions and they
get to pay the consequence or to enjoy the fruits of their decisions. That's the way the system works."—Treasury Secretary
Paul O'Neill, on the collapse of Enron, which cost thousands
of people their jobs, their pensions, their life savings. ABC
Radio (1/15/02).

"It's very important for folks to understand that when there's
more trade, there's more commerce."—President George W.
Bush, Quebec City, Quebec, Canada (4/21/01).[1]

"He [Bush] opens his mouth, and the market goes down. I'm
not saying he's responsible for the market crash. But he hasn't
inspired a rush for investors to get back in."—Stephen Moore,
Club for Growth, *New York Times* (8/12/02).

"With the economy wobbling and the stock market roiling, the
President badly needs the A-team of economic advisors. . . .
Unfortunately, he doesn't have one. He barely has a C-team,
when it's functioning at all." *Fortune* (9/2/02).

"I mean, these good folks are revolutionizing how businesses
conduct their business. And, like them, I am very optimistic
about our position in the world and about its influence on
the United States. . . . And so, I hope investors, you know—
secondly, I hope investors hold investments for periods of
time—that I've always found the best investments are those
that you salt away based on economics."—George W. Bush,
Austin, Texas (1/4/01).[2]

"I'm constantly amazed that anybody cares what I do."
—Treasury Secretary Paul O'Neill.[3]

"The world fears that Karl Rove now controls U.S. international economic policy."—David Hale, Economist, Zurich Group.[4]

"The United States appears to have slipped into an economic funk that analysts say bears a strong resemblance to the weak recovery of the early 1990s. With few companies adding jobs and Americans' net worth having dropped more than 20 percent in the last two years, the coming months are likely to feel like a slump even if the economy is gradually improving." *New York Times* (8/12/02).

"We're heading in the right direction."—President George W. Bush, 7/31/02, quoted in the *New York Times* (8/2/02).

"Can't anybody here play this game?" Manager Casey Stengel to the 1962 New York Mets.[5]

George Herbert Hoover Bush

Even the most dedicated Bush apologists, many of whom are quoted here, admit that the Bush economic team has been a failure. But—as Mike Dukakis once said about another administration—"a fish rots from the head down."

There's no doubt the Bush economic team is weak. And the weakness begins with the team's leader: Bush himself. The *New York Times* analyzed Bush's counterproductive attempts to shape the economy, concluding, "his words have often had the opposite effect than he intended, sometimes seeming to send the financial markets diving."[6]

Sometimes? The *Times* is too kind. Consider this scorecard from just one month—July 2002.

- July 9, 2002: Bush gives a major address on Wall Street. The subject: corporate accountability. His aides had told reporters before the speech that they'd hoped Bush's words would rally stocks.[7] Instead, the Dow fell 178.81 the day

Bush spoke, and dropped a total of almost 700 points the
week of Bush's speech.[8]

- July 22, 2002: Bush forcefully defends his treasury secretary,
  Paul O'Neill. Then, suddenly becoming a market analyst—
  and a bull at that—Bush says, "there is value in the market
  now." The Dow drops 234.68 points—2.9 percent—in a single day.[9]

- July 30, 2002: Bush signs a major anti-corporate-fraud bill
  (one whose provisions he'd opposed). The market, unimpressed, barely budges.[10]

- July 31, 2002: The Commerce Department reports that the
  nation's gross domestic product grew by 1.1 percent the
  previous quarter, down from 5 percent in the first three
  months of the year. Bush boasts, "We're heading in the right
  direction."[11]

Something serious is going on. Americans have lost $4.4 trillion
in stock-market investments since George W. Bush took office. Not
since Herbert Hoover presided over the Crash of 1929 has an American president seen the stock market fall so dramatically in his first
eighteen months in office.[12]

No serious person believes the president controls the daily fluc-
tuations of the stock market, but a wise president (like Bill Clinton)
knows better than to act as if he does.

Even strong Bush supporters are openly critical of his economic
stewardship. Sen. Chuck Hagel of Nebraska has an 82 percent rating
from the American Conservative Union. And yet this conservative
Republican had this to say about Bush's utter lack of competence on
the economy: "He [Bush] obviously has not been very effective. People knew when they listened to Clinton that there was something behind him. There was Bob Rubin, there was an economic team. I don't
think the markets see anything behind this president's words."[13]

Hagel isn't alone. His fellow conservative, Club for Growth president Stephen Moore, told the *New York Times*, "He opens his mouth,
and the markets go down. I'm not saying he's responsible for the

Those Who Can't, Meet

They were holed up in a heavily armed compound in Waco, surrounded by federal agents. Only true believers were allowed within the walls of the compound and, as groupthink took hold, even the most banal comments from the cult's leader were treated as wisdom.

The Branch Davidians? No, the Bush economic summit.

Dubya gathered Americans from all walks of life—especially if you do a lot of walking with corporate CEOs, special-interest lobbyists and major Bush campaign donors. And just to keep the spirit of the event completely Republican, Charles Schwab, CEO of the eponymous investment company, laid off 400 workers as he lectured the rest of us about the economy.[14]

So, while layoff artists were included, critics of Bush's failed economic policies, members of Congress and anyone else who might have the temerity to point out that Dubya's economic policies aren't working, were excluded.

As the *New York Times* reported, "Mr. Bush heard no dissent and no debate at an event where the theme was that the economy was going through difficulty, but that things were headed in the right direction. The forum has been heavily criticized by the Democrats and a number of Republicans as a staged pep rally for the second Bush White House, which is ever mindful of the fate of Mr. Bush's father. Former President Bush was enormously popular after the Persian Gulf war but lost the 1992 election in large part because of voters' perceptions that he no longer had control of the economy."[15]

Suggesting that the session was scripted by the White House, the *Times* reported that "Karl Rove, the president's chief political adviser, said after the forum that he was 'not aware' that the White House had supplied the participants talking points, but 'that's not to say there weren't any.' "[16]

★———★———★———★———★———★———★———★

Bruce Bartlett, an economic adviser to former Presidents Reagan and Bush, was more candid than Karl about the canned event. He told the conservative *Washington Times* that the forum "may help break the monotony of an otherwise dreary morning in the dog days of August. But the likelihood that anything worthwhile will be achieved is close to zero. It is just a complete waste of the president's time and it will accomplish absolutely nothing."[17]

Afterward, pulling back the curtain and admitting to the artifice, Bush thanked the people at Baylor University for, "putting on a great show."[18]

Bush was so pleased with the criticism-free sessions that he's thinking of having future summits on what a great dancer he is and how his public speaking is reminiscent of Winston Churchill.

The markets, however, were not as impressed with Dubya as he was with himself. Stocks fell as Bush tried to display his mastery of economic policy—sitting as long as 20 whole minutes at a time during some sessions—with the Dow dropping 206.43 to close at 8,482.46.[19]

The whole event—Bush looking trapped and over his head, Cheney stifling yawns, corporate big shots shamelessly sucking up—had a vaguely Stalinist feel to it: government officials and corporate bosses being forced to praise the demonstrably failed economic policies of the current regime, state-sanctioned slogans assaulting us at every camera angle, and the Worshipful Leader's every platitude received with reverence.

Bush didn't sit through the day-long affair, but he promised to read the highlights later. Right. Maureen Dowd of the *Times* had dubbed Dubya's tenure "the Cliff Notes presidency."[20] In case you didn't get your White House, whitewashed summary of the proceedings, the good folks at a website called www.liberaloasis.com have compiled some of the highlights for you. Now you, too, can be like our president and peruse only what others think is valuable for you to know. Here are quotes that liberaloasis.com pulled from the White House transcript of the summit.

DUBYA: I can assure you that, even though I won't be sitting through every single moment of the seminars, nor will the Vice President, we will look at the summaries . . .

DUBYA: There may be some tough times here in America. But this country has gone through tough times before, and we're going to do it again.

DUBYA: You ought to take a look at—Franklin can tell you, the government accounting system is pretty—it's kind of hard to explain. I've been there for nearly 18 months trying to figure it out.

DUBYA: In order to make sure that we continue to grow our economy, we need to be aggressive when it comes to trade policy. [U.S. Trade Representative Bob] Zoellick mentioned to me, he said they're all looking to me. They may be looking to me, Zoellick, I'm looking to you.

BUDGET DIRECTOR MITCH DANIELS: The question is did we hear any ideas today that might become policy. The answer is, I don't know yet.

DUBYA: It's really a fine seminar because the quality of the people are great. Wait until you see who's here when you go to lunch. It's really impressed.

COMMERCE SECRETARY DON EVANS: I thought it was an extraordinary morning. I was in the corporate responsibility section. The President did stop by. There was a lot of engagement.

DUBYA: I now believe we ought to have medical liability reform at the federal level . . . The trial lawyers are

★   ★   ★   ★   ★   ★   ★   ★

> very politically powerful . . . but here in Texas we took
> them on and got some good medical—medical malprac-
> tice, which evidently had a few loopholes in it.
>
> **DUBYA:** Tommy [Thompson, Health and Human Ser-
> vices Secretary] is a good listener, and he's a pretty good
> actor, too.
>
> **EVANS:** Well, the economy—we continue to—we con-
> tinue to add jobs to this economy, not in large numbers,
> but we're adding jobs.
>
> **DUBYA:** I promise you I will listen to what has been said
> here, even though I wasn't here.[21]
>
> With all this economic uncertainty, I don't want to make it
> more difficult for you to sleep at night. I really don't. But once
> you realize how massively incompetent Bush and his economic
> team are, you'll sleep like a baby—waking up every two hours
> to cry and wet the bed.

market crash. But he hasn't inspired a rush for investors to get back
in."[22] When the country needed strong economic leadership after
9/11, Moore said, "There's a sense that the White House is providing
almost no economic leadership."[23]

Folks are resorting to gallows humor, saying their 401(k)'s have become "201(k)'s," and that their IRAs are now IOUs. Pennsylvania Democratic congressional candidate (and my old pal) Dan Wofford told me
about a pit bull in Phoenixville, Pennsylvania, who'd chewed through
the screen of the front porch window, snarling and threatening the
candidate as he campaigned door-to-door. Unfazed, Wofford said he
understood. "The dog's probably angry about losing his 401-Canine."

The Keystone Kops

The business magazine *Fortune* published a scathing critique of the
Bush economic team in its September 2, 2002, issue. *Fortune* head-
lined the article, "The Gang That Couldn't Shoot Straight," and

plainly asserted that Bush's team is not up to the task of guiding the government through difficult economic times. "With the economy wobbling and the stock market roiling, the President badly needs the A-team of economic advisors. Unfortunately . . . he doesn't have one. He barely has a C-team, when it's functioning at all. Its members are tone-deaf to Main Street, Wall Street, and Capitol Hill—in some cases defiantly so. . . . Now is the moment Paul O'Neill, Pitt, Commerce Secretary Don Evans, White House economic aide Larry Lindsey, and Bush's other top [advisors] need to prove that they aren't the Keystone Kops of federal finance."[24]

Ouch. And lest you think that was written by some liberal anti-Bush hack, think again. It was penned by none other than Jeffrey Birnbaum who, in addition to writing for *Fortune*, is a paid commentator on the right-wing Fox News Network. Birnbaum is viewed as such a thoroughly pro-Bush writer that, back in Texas, Birnbaum was chided by the *Texas Observer* for composing the following love letter to Dubya: "A reformed carouser who speaks with the zeal of the converted, George W. is more passionate, more spiritual, more substantive, more charming, more quick-tempered, more wily, more witty, more conservative, and politically more astute than George H. W. ever was. Don't expect him to tell people to read his lips."[25]

When a reporter who once called Bush "substantive"—indeed, more substantive than his Phi Beta Kappa father—begins to turn on him, you know Junior is in what Poppy would have called (in his unsubstantive way) "deep doo-doo."

While Bush is clearly responsible for his policies and the team he put in place to enact them, it would be tough to pick the MDP—most damaging player. But let's try.

Vice President (and former CEO) Dick Cheney

The continuing controversy surrounding alleged accounting irregularities at Halliburton have largely sidelined the most influential unelected, court-appointed vice president in history. He didn't even show up for the all-hands-on-deck signing of the Democratic anti-corporate-corruption bill—a bill whose key provisions Cheney (and Bush, for that matter) had bitterly opposed. *Fortune*'s Birnbaum analyzes Cheney's contribution to the economic team thusly: "Cheney has already hurt Bush more than is widely known. The Vice President's deeply conservative opinions, which served him well in the War on Terror, have hindered the War on Corporate Misconduct. As Bush's most trusted counselor, Cheney was instrumental in preventing the President from coming down more harshly on financial miscreants."[26]

Secretary of the Treasury (and former CEO) Paul O'Neill

People who know Paul O'Neill (and I'm not one of them) invariably describe him as brilliant. People who have analyzed his performance as treasury secretary have had to dig a little deeper into their thesaurus. Words like *erratic*, *gaffe prone*, and *shoot from the lip* surface repeatedly.

The long list of unhelpful, insensitive or downright stupid things Secretary O'Neill has said is large and growing. Here are just a few:

O'Neill criticized efforts by Democrats to help workers unemployed in the wake of September 11 subsidize their health-insurance premiums with tax credits. O'Neill said the Democratic plan, "was a huge reach and change in policy, putting the federal government into a position where it's now going to create a new entitlement class." The *New York Times* reported that the Bush administration plans to veto such a plan.[27] Only a multimillionaire, Republican CEO like O'Neill could look at the possibility of 638,312 workers laid off because of the terrorist attacks losing their health care and call them "a new entitlement class."[28]

Similarly, O'Neill seemed to revel in the collapse of Enron. "Companies come and go," he said. "Part of the genius of capitalism is people get to make good decisions or bad decisions and they get to pay the consequence or to enjoy the fruits of their decisions. That's the way the system works."[29] Thousands of people had lost their jobs, their savings, their retirement, their investments—all through no fault of their own. Anyone else would have seen havoc and heartbreak. O'Neill saw "the genius of capitalism."

I guess that's what they call "compassionate conservatism."

A sensitive man, our treasury secretary once barked at the *New York Times*, "If people don't like what I'm doing, I don't give a damn."[30]

If O'Neill lacks empathy for the common man, he certainly has plenty for the poor, benighted corporations of the world. In an interview with the *Financial Times*, O'Neill announced that he wanted to abolish the corporate income and capital gains tax on businesses. "Not only am I committed to working on this issue, the president is also intrigued about the possibility of fixing this mess," O'Neill said.[31]

The "mess" O'Neill was referring to is the fact that corporations sometimes actually have to pay taxes. If O'Neill and Bush had their way, corporations would pay no taxes at all. Who would make up the revenue? You got it, bud. People. One of the enduring goals of Bushonomics is to shift the burden of taxation away from corporations and onto people.

One of the charming things about O'Neill is his candor. He thinks health care for people who lost their jobs due to the September 11 attacks is welfare, and he says so. He doesn't think corporations should be taxed, and he says so. Bush is more cagey. He pretends to be on the side of working folks, loves to talk about the men and women at the coffee shop in Crawford, Texas—then he pushes policies that nail them to the wall.

O'Neill's politically incorrect outbursts must drive Bush crazy, but perhaps nothing drove Junior more batty than when O'Neill actually slipped up and told the truth about tax cuts. According to *Newsweek*, "as the Treasury secretary admits, the [Bush tax cut] plan isn't an anti-recession tool."[32]

The emperor has no clothes! The Bush tax cut was not an antirecession tool. Of course, we now know this because Congress enacted the Bush tax cut for the rich and we had a recession anyway, but to hear it from the mouth of the Bush administration's point man on economic policy really is extraordinary.

Bush shouldn't have been shocked by O'Neill's candor on taxes. During his confirmation hearing, O'Neill said he didn't believe tax cuts would work to help business investments: "I never made an investment decision based on the tax code. . . . You know, maybe I should say more directly to you, if you're giving money away, I'll take it. You know, if you want to give me inducements for something I'm going to do anyway, I'll take it. But good business people don't do things because of inducements."[33]

After taking office, O'Neill continued to pull back the curtain on the phony rationale Bush gave for his tax cut for the rich. Whereas

Dubya maintained that "the key thing is that we have meaningful, real tax relief, where everybody who pays taxes gets relief, and where, to the best extent possible, accelerate the tax relief to get money in people's pockets to serve as a stimulus to the economy,"[34] O'Neill admitted that the tax cut would not stimulate the economy. During a private meeting with a group of two dozen moderate Democratic and Republican senators, O'Neill "bluntly stated that the slowly phased-in, six-year tax reduction plan is not 'stimulative enough in the first years.' " According to an op-ed piece in the ultraconservative *Washington Times* by Donald Lambro, "Mr. O'Neill—who has voiced deep doubts about whether fiscal policy can provide any immediate stimulus to the economy—remarked, 'Look, I'll be in trouble if this gets out.' "[35]

O'Neill committed the sin of candor again several months later when he blasted the House GOP stimulus package as "show business."[36] He was right, but the next day Bush endorsed the House GOP package.[37] So if the stimulus package was show business, George W. Bush was Ethel Merman.

O'Neill's bluntness may be refreshing when he's admitting that Bush's tax cuts are nothing more than a handout to the idle rich, and Bush's stimulus package was phony, but it's downright dangerous in other venues. Twice within five weeks in the summer of 2002 he insulted the nation of Brazil, ridiculed reform efforts there and sent its currency into a nosedive. First, he criticized an important International Monetary Fund loan to Brazil, calling it "political." The Brazilian markets, already jittery from the strong campaigns of leftist candidates, swooned. Cooler heads at the Treasury Department stepped in, issued an apologetic statement, and said the U.S. has confidence in Brazil's economic management.[38]

Then, five weeks later, appearing on *Fox News Sunday*, O'Neill again launched a gratuitous broadside against Brazil—and insulted Argentina and Uruguay in the process. Ever the diplomat, O'Neill said the key to financial assistance to struggling Latin American economies is to make sure the money "doesn't just go out of the country to Swiss bank accounts."[39]

This time, O'Neill's mess was too big for the Treasury press operation to handle. Ari Fleischer himself, accustomed to cleaning up after Dubya, but no doubt annoyed to be changing Paul O'Neill's diapers, had to set things right. O'Neill's big mouth had—literally—caused an international incident.[40]

O'Neill is target number one for the Republicans. Stephen Moore of the Club for Growth gave voice to what many others in his party say privately: "Bush needs to reassign Paul O'Neill to some other job in the administration and get a more effective spokesman for economic policy," he told the *New York Times*.[41] Another Republican—this one wouldn't let the *Times* use his name—said, "There are a lot of people who would like to see him gone in the next half hour."[42]

All of this is a little unfair, if you ask me. The chief criticisms of O'Neill are that he sometimes commits verbal gaffes and that he lacks gravitas.

Helllllllllllooooooo?

If Bush is going to start getting rid of people who are gaffe prone and lack gravitas he'd better start writing his own resignation speech.

"It's not that he's bad, and it's not that he's dumb," a New York banker who attended a meeting with O'Neill told *Time*. "It's just that he has no gravitas. And once you lose it, you can't get it back."[43]

No, you can't, sir. No, you can't. And neither can our president. He can fire Paul O'Neill. But the buck doesn't stop at the Treasury Department.

The Keystone Kops: The Rest of the Bush Economic Team

The Keystone Kops were a creation of film pioneer Mack Sennett. Although their heyday was 85 years ago, the name lives on. The specialty of the Keystone Kops was *slapstick*—physical comedy. Pratfalls, car wrecks, hilarious (and dangerous) stunts, including jumping out of moving cars—and, of course, the pie in the face—were their hallmarks. Part of what made the Kops so funny, and so enduring (as opposed, say, to the Keystone Firemen) is that as police officers, the Kops were authority figures. And there's something hilarious about watching authority figures smash into each other, clueless and comedic.[44]

When the authority figures are supposed to be managing America's economic policy, it's not quite so funny when they bump into each other.

According to the *Washington Post*, "Over the months, there have been tensions between Lindsey and O'Neill, in part because of O'Neill's penchant for provocative statements and Lindsey's desire to gain better control over the process, as well as the natural proclivity of Treasury and White House aides to battle for supremacy over policy."[45]

The *Los Angeles Times* reported, "[T]he administration's key economic policymakers—Daniels, Treasury Secretary Paul H. O'Neill, chief economic advisor Lawrence B. Lindsey and R. Glenn Hubbard, chairman of the president's Council of Economic Advisers—appear to have ad-libbed much of the early response [to 9/11 relief]. The result has been a series of mix-ups in which one official appeared to contradict another. Early on, for example, O'Neill counseled that Congress should go slow in approving relief measures, while Lindsey called for bold action. As recently as Tuesday, Daniels and O'Neill had trouble hiding their distaste for the size of the House's $100-billion stimulus package, while more political operatives such as Fleischer seemed ready to accept it."[46]

The *New York Times* editorialized: "With Congress beginning to debate a possible stimulus package this week, the White House has been surprisingly silent on how seriously it regards the current economic situation, or what it wants to do to improve it. Treasury Secretary Paul O'Neill and the rest of the Bush team have yet to show full command of the issues they face. . . . Americans are waiting for Mr. Bush to take command of the economy and show that he can adapt to changed circumstances and fashion a program that favors immediate need over ideology. If the president's current advisers are not up to the job of reassuring the nation, Mr. Bush needs to improve his bench."[47]

Bush and the Bumblers have argued publicly among themselves on a host of issues, one contradicting the other, a cacophony of incompetence. They couldn't get their act together on economic stimulus. On one day, Council of Economic Advisers Chairman R. Glenn Hubbard said the economy could recover without an economic stimulus package,[48] while on the same day President Bush called for stimulus "as quickly as possible."[49]

Similarly, while National Economic Council Chairman Larry Lindsey flatly stated on November 9, 2001 that "if we hadn't had September 11, it's quite clear the economy would have avoided a recession,"[50] he was contradicted five days later by Vice President Cheney. Cheney told the U.S. Chamber of Commerce that the economy was headed to "recessionary levels" even before the terrorist attacks.[51] And, to add to the scrum, a few days later Secretary O'Neill said "our economy was beginning to show real growth rates again in July and August and in the first ten days of September,"[52]—a zig-zag-zig that contradicted Cheney and underscored the lack of any coherent sense of economic reality, much less economic strategy.

Sometimes you only need one Kop to have a wreck. On October 6, 2001, CEA Chair Glenn Hubbard appeared on CNN's *Novak, Hunt & Shields,* and announced: "It's certainly true that the president has said he remains open to talking about a minimum wage increase."[53] Just a few days later, the *Washington Post* reported that a leading economic spokesman for the Bush administration had shot that notion down; he "spelled out the administration's position on increasing the minimum wage: 'No.' "[54] Who was the administration official who so coldly contradicted Glenn Hubbard? Why, none other than Dr. Hubbard himself.

I gotta hand it to the Bushies. Even the most inventive of the Keystone Kops never thought to smash a pie in his *own* face.

The Top Financial Cop:
More Like Barney Fife than Dirty Harry

No discussion of the Bush economic team would be complete without mention of Harvey Pitt. As Bush's handpicked chairman of the Securities and Exchange Commission, Pitt is the man responsible for policing the financial markets. Before becoming the top financial cop, Pitt was the leading lawyer for all (yes, all) of the Big Six (now Big Four) accounting firms.[55] In that capacity, he was the leading force *opposing* President Clinton's proposals to prevent corporate fraud. Choosing Harvey Pitt to patrol financial crooks is like hiring John Gotti's lawyer to run the FBI.

As the *Los Angeles Times* commented in a prescient editorial early in his tenure, "The new SEC chairman, Harvey L. Pitt, may unfortunately be the accounting firms' best friend. A lawyer who formerly represented the accounting industry, he dismisses as hysteria the critics' warnings about accountants' conflicts of interest and poor practices. It's up to Congress to keep the SEC on track or risk more hidden corporate misdeeds that will eventually be laid at government's door."[56]

In his first official speech as SEC chairman, Pitt spoke to the American Institute of Certified Public Accountants—itself a former client of Pitt's. Pitt's appearance alone was noteworthy, as Pitt's predecessor, Clinton appointee Arthur Levitt, had fought the accountants—and Pitt himself—over Levitt's desire to separate auditing functions from lucrative consulting contracts. Levitt believed that an auditing firm serving as a paid consultant to a corporation was a built-in conflict of interest. (The disgraceful behavior of Arthur Andersen in the Enron case proved Levitt right.)

Harvey Pitt is no Arthur Levitt. And that's the point he wanted to make to his former clients in the accounting industry. He began his speech by noting that, "To put a fine point on it, as accountants often say, the agency I am privileged to lead has not, of late, always been a kinder and gentler place for accountants; and the audit profession, in turn, has not always had nice things to say about us!"[57] Later in the speech he said, "At the Commission, we view the accounting profession as our partner. . . ."[58]

Pitt defenders have claimed that the much-publicized and widely criticized "kinder gentler" comment was taken out of context, that Pitt was only joking.

Horsefeathers.

Pitt wanted to tell his former clients that, unlike that mean Arthur Levitt, Uncle Harvey was not going to be a hard-ass when it came to strictly enforcing the law where accountants were concerned. He called for "a continuing dialogue, and partnership, with the accounting profession," and pledged to "do everything in our power to evidence a new era of respect and cooperation."[59] Of course, he had one boilerplate sentence about fraud—just one in the entire speech—but the point of the speech was unmistakable. There was a new sheriff in town. And he acted a lot like Barney Fife.

Pitt wasted little time in defanging America's most important corporate watchdog. In August 2001, soon after Pitt assumed his role as chairman of the SEC, the agency's staff stopped work on a report that indicated severe shortcomings in the accounting industry's peer review system, under which accounting firms review each others' work every three years. The SEC found that despite major flaws in the way audits were conducted, the auditing firms gave each other clean bills of health. The aborted SEC report also was to have included recommendations for bolstering oversight of the accounting industry that, according to the *Wall Street Journal*, "would have differed significantly from the plan Mr. Pitt outlined Jan. 17 for overhauling auditor supervision. . . ." SEC spokeswoman Christi Harlan said the project "just petered out" with the change of administrations.[60]

I wouldn't say it "petered out," Ms. Harlan. I'd say it was Pitted.

Controversy and allegations of conflict of interest continue to dog Pitt. In April 2002, Pitt met with the head of one of the largest accounting firms, KPMG CEO Eugene O'Kelly. The meeting raised eyebrows because, at the time, KPMG's audits of Xerox were being investigated by the SEC. In an e-mail O'Kelly distributed to his staff, he said that he had met privately with Pitt and—as the *New York Times* reported—"He forcefully criticized an SEC investigation of the firm for its work for Xerox."[61]

Pitt admitted the meeting had taken place, but described it as a courtesy call from the new CEO of KPMG and insisted that the Xerox case had never been discussed. Discussing an ongoing enforcement action with a former client would have violated ethics rules. O'Kelly later sent a letter to inquiring lawmakers, backpedaling from his earlier claim, and essentially agreeing with Pitt that the meeting had been social.[62] Some Congressmen were unimpressed. Rep. Ed Markey (D-MA) said, "Last week Mr. O'Kelly acknowledged that he had 'referenced a potential proceeding against the firm.' Now, Mr. O'Kelly says the Xerox matter never specifically came up. Which account are we to believe? We still haven't gotten to the bottom of this and I don't like the smell of it."[63]

Even if you take Pitt at his word, the meeting was a mistake. As Charles Lewis of the Center for Public Integrity put it, "It seems like he [Pitt] meets with whomever he wants, regardless of circumstances, past professional relationships or the fact that they might be under investigation by his own agency. To say it's playing things fast and loose is an understatement."[64]

Ill-advised meetings have become something of a habit for Mr. Pitt. In December 2001, Pitt met privately with corporate accountants to develop a new accounting oversight board. When those meetings became known, the entire existing supervisory board resigned in protest.[65]

Pitt was also criticized for not formally recusing himself from the SEC probe of Enron, because its auditor, Arthur Andersen, was another former Pitt client.[66]

The fox assures us all is well in the henhouse.

As if that weren't enough, Pitt—a well-fed, well-paid, multimillionaire, fat cat lawyer—actually had the *cojones* to ask for a raise. A 21 percent raise. And a seat in the president's cabinet, which means he would outrank the director of the Central Intelligence Agency, directors of the Environmental Protection Agency and the National Aeronautics and Space Administration.[67]

In Texas, we call that *chutzpah.*

The Bottom Line

I want to apologize to the 1962 New York Mets for comparing them to the Bush economic team. Sure, the Mets went 40–120, a record for losses that still stands today. And sure their best pitcher—their best, mind you—*lost* 24 games. But that pitcher, Roger Craig, went on to be a good big-league manager. And other members of the '62 Mets weren't bad either. Don Zimmer, the third baseman, is bench coach/ Yoda/good luck charm/guru for the Yankees, having spent all his adult life in baseball. Center fielder Richie Ashburn is in the Hall of Fame. And ex-Dodger Gil Hodges, who played first base on that first Met team, managed the Mets to their miracle World Series championship in 1969.

I also want to apologize to the Keystone Kops. They're all dead now, so I should more properly address my apologies to their memories and their heirs. The mayhem of the Keystone Kops was intentional, the catastrophes choreographed.

Not so with the Bush economic team. Years from now, no one will look back on the Bush economic team with such fondness. Their incompetence, their inadequacy, their ineptitude, their inconstancy, their ignorance of the real lives of real people is staggering.

Junior could fire any of them or all of them, however, and nothing will change.

Until we fire Junior.

ELEVEN

What the Democrats Are For (Or at Least What They Should Be For)

THIS BOOK, IN CASE YOU HAVEN'T YET GUESSED, IS NOT A POLICY PRE-scription to cure what ails us. Rather, it's a catalog of what's gone wrong. A compendium of the many mistaken and wrongheaded economic decisions made by the Only President We Have.

Listing the faults of the current regime before detailing what should replace it is a tradition at least as old as America itself. Our Founding Fathers had a two-stage process—first a Declaration of Independence that served as a list of grievances, then a Constitution that set out the nuts and bolts of the new order for the ages.

In other words, somebody's got to yell "Fire!" before anybody will run for the hose. The purpose of this book is to yell "Fire!"

Still, I can't resist including at least a few broad policy objectives that I believe the Democratic Party ought to stand for.

The Law of Holes

The First Law of Holes, of course, says that when you find yourself in a hole, stop digging. So, the first, most obvious step we can take is to call an immediate halt to Bushonomics. Some congressional Democrats believe the way to do this is to force President Bush into a budget summit, much as they did to his father in 1990. (For those of you too young to remember, Bush Senior agreed to a tax increase at a budget summit at Andrews Air Force Base. That's when Senior broke his read-my-lips pledge and raised taxes.)

What those congressional Democrats don't seem to understand is that, for reasons even Dr. Freud would take a lifetime to fathom, Junior is at least as determined to do things differently from his dad as he is committed to doing everything 180 degrees differently from Clinton. So, the mere fact that Poppy agreed to raise taxes in the face of a crushing deficit should not lead anyone to the conclusion that Junior will do the same. Indeed, if my amateur psychology is correct, the fact that Poppy raised taxes means it's a dead-solid certainty that Junior won't back away from his tax cut for the rich. (Junior, who never was strong at economics, continues to assert, falsely, that foreswearing a promised tax cut is the same thing as a tax increase. It's not, and anyone with a brain knows that, but don't hold your breath waiting for Dubya to grasp that simple fact.)

Democrats have to stand for something. And we have a model: the most successful economic strategy since Franklin Roosevelt saved us from the Great Depression: the Clinton Economic Strategy. Clinton's economic strategy rested on three pillars: fiscal discipline, free trade, and investing in people. Democrats should challenge Bush on all three fronts.

Put the Bush Tax Cut in the Deep Freeze

Democrats need an alternative tax strategy. Too many of them look like they don't know whether to scratch their watch or wind their ass. But this is not a hard call. Bush's tax cut is so irresponsible, so damaging, so tilted toward the moneyed elite, that blocking its final implementation should be our top priority.

I'd leave in place the first phase of the Bush tax cut. The $300 rebates many Americans received were better than a poke in the eye with a sharp stick, but three-quarters of all Americans have already gotten everything they're going to get from the Bush tax cut. The second phase of the tax cut is a gift to the most prosperous 1 percent— who'll get $53,123 a year from Dubya once his entire tax cut is completely phased in.[1]

So, most Americans won't lose anything if we freeze the Bush tax cut right where it is. And, in fact, the top 1 percent will be better off without the tax cut, too. Any rich person with a brain knows they did a hell of a lot better under Clinton's economy—even with a tax *increase* on the rich—than they're doing in the Bush recession. The best way for the rich to get even richer is to have a growing economy, and the Bush deficits—caused by the Bush tax cuts—are the biggest drain on our long-term economic health. Former Treasury Secretary Bob Rubin—someone who actually knows something about economic stewardship—made the case in an op-ed piece in the *Washington Post:* "Long-term fiscal discipline and a sound long-term fiscal position contribute substantially, over time but also in the short term, to lower interest rates, increased consumer and business confidence, and to attracting much-needed capital from abroad to our savings-deficient country. In addition, a sound long-term fiscal position would far better enable us to meet our long-term Social Security and Medicare commitments."[2]

Democrats should call for freezing the Bush tax cut immediately. No one will have to give back anything they've been given, so no honest person can claim it's a tax increase. But none of us will get the second part of the tax cut: the part that's going to do the most fiscal and economic damage; the part that's most heavily tilted toward the well-off; the part that will make it impossible for America to gain control of its fiscal policy for a generation or more.

Save Social Security First

As I argued in the chapter on tax cuts—and again when we discussed Social Security (sorry if this is redundant, but it is a *very big deal*)—over the next 75 years the Bush tax cut will drain $8.7 trillion in revenue from the government. The entire shortfall in Social Security in the same period is just $3.7 trillion.[3] So, if you were to follow President Clinton's mandate and save Social Security first by freezing the Bush tax cuts and plowing some of the savings into the Social Security Trust Fund, you could guarantee that Social Security benefits will not be reduced, nor Social Security taxes increased, nor will the Social Security Trust Fund be exhausted until well after 2077—and still have trillions left over.

Let me be clear about what that means. It means that all the dire, doomsday predictions of all the blue-ribbon panels and the pontificating editorialists are wrong. If we have the wisdom to freeze

Dubya's wrongheaded tax cuts, and invest that money in the Social Security Trust Fund, we'll have more than enough money to save Social Security. It means the Social Security system will be solvent until the last of the baby boomers (those born in 1964) are at least 113. So, I hope those of you born in 1964 eat right and exercise. 'Cause if we freeze Dubya's tax increase there will be more than enough in the Social Security Trust Fund to pay your benefits till you think of 100-year-olds as young whippersnappers.

Tax Cuts that Create Jobs and Help Working Families

In analyzing the Bush tax policy, we saw that Dubya likes to cut those taxes that are disproportionately paid by the most prosperous, while ignoring the kinds of taxes that fall most heavily on working people. Democrats should stand that policy on its head.

Democrats should call for a reduction in the payroll tax. Eighty percent of us pay more in payroll taxes than in income taxes, so for four out of five Americans, a payroll tax cut would be a more meaningful tax cut.[4] The money we would save from freezing Bush's income tax cut would more than make up for any lost revenue to the Social Security Trust Fund, which is financed by the payroll tax.

Cutting the payroll tax has another virtue that income tax cuts don't have: it would be a job generator, big time. Because payroll taxes are matched by employers, a cut in the payroll tax would also be a cut in the taxes businesses pay. Our high payroll taxes act as a drag on new hires, so cutting them would give businesses—large and small—a powerful new way to reduce their labor costs and expand employment without cutting wages.

I'd trade income tax cuts for payroll tax cuts any day of the week. A payroll tax cut allows Democrats once again to be true to our heritage, to be the party of people who work hard for a living, the party of struggling small businessmen and women, the party of economic growth and an expanding pie.

Reinstate the Estate Tax; Cut the Pre-Death Tax

You already know by now that more than 98 percent of us will never pay the estate tax.[5] Bush's effort to repeal it is class warfare at its worst—the wealthiest few families in America trying to avoid paying any taxes at all on money they get from being smart enough to choose very, very wealthy parents.

But what's this *pre-death tax?* It's the name the economist Robert Kuttner and the political scientist Michael Lipsky have given to the Medicaid spend-down rule, which requires seniors to spend themselves into poverty before they're eligible for Medicaid long-term care. Kuttner, coeditor of *The American Prospect,* notes that while almost none of us will pay the estate tax, nearly all of us run the risk of being wiped out by the pre-death tax.

"Nursing home care," Kuttner has written, "typically costs a resident about $60,000 a year, and it costs the country as a whole about $90 billion. In 1998, Medicaid paid just under half, and people paying out of pocket covered about one third."[6] But before you can qualify for Medicaid, you've got to be basically broke.

Medicaid, you see, is a program designed for the poor. And yet it pays the lion's share of long-term health care costs for our seniors— because the pre-death tax forces them to spend their life savings. It is not uncommon for an older American to work her whole life, amass a nest egg of $250,000 (not a penny of which would be subject to the estate tax), then see it all disappear to cover four or five years of long-term health care.

Eliminating the pre-death tax would allow seniors to keep their savings, leave it to their children or grandchildren, their church or charity, and still receive long-term care without being reduced to pauperdom. Such a system of long-term care would not be cheap; Kuttner estimates it would cost $30 billion a year.[7] The good news is, that's about half what it will cost us to permanently abolish the estate tax.

"In other words," Kuttner argues, "we could entirely get rid of the pre-death tax on middle-class people, if we simply chose not to abolish the estate tax on the wealthy. We could earmark proceeds of the estate tax for long-term nursing home care for all, under Medicare."[8]

This is why God (or at least Tom Jefferson and Andy Jackson) made the Democratic Party. If we can't stand up for tax cuts that help senior citizens live with dignity, and a sensible estate tax that only the richest—and deadest—1.6 percent of us will ever pay, there's no point in being a Democrat.

Free Trade—and Real Help for Steel

One of the most crassly cynical moves of the Bush presidency was Dubya's decision to slap protectionist tariffs on steel and lumber. Many analysts saw the moves as naked politics—pandering to steelworkers in the key swing states of the Midwest and timbermen in the Northwest and the South. I have no idea what Bush's motive was. But I know this: His embrace of trade protectionism was an act of breathtaking hypocrisy.

In a speech to the Council of the Americas on May 7, 2001, the Only President We Have said: "Open trade is not just an economic opportunity, it is a moral imperative."[9]

A moral imperative. Wow. Dubya had clearly been up late the night before rereading what must be one of his favorite books, Immanuel Kant's 1785 masterpiece, *Grundlegung zur Metaphysik der Sitten*. A man with two Ivy League degrees, Bush doubtless was reading it in the original German. We state-school plebeians know it in English as *Grounding for the Metaphysics of Morals*.[10] In it, Kant attempts to articulate laws of moral philosophy that have the same utility as the physical laws (gravity, motion, thermodynamics and the like).

As our Ivy League president no doubt knows, Kant was searching for a morality that was not grounded in appeals to God or community or threat of punishment, but rather in reason. He describes a *moral imperative* as an act free from ulterior motives, something that one simply must do. As Kant himself put it: "Act only according to that maxim by which you can at the same time will that it should become a universal law."[11] In other words, don't just do X because you personally believe it's the right thing to do. Do X because you believe the entire world should do so as well. Do X because, if you were king of the world, you'd make it a universal law that everyone must do X, in the same way that gravity is a universal physical law that must be obeyed by everything on earth. There can be no exceptions. No moral person can do otherwise.[12]

Of course, I'm not the philosopher Bush is. But I do know this: a moral imperative is a very big deal. It's not just the preferred public policy or the superior economic policy. It's not even the better moral course. It's the *only* moral course.

Imagine my surprise when our philosopher president abandoned free trade after calling it a "moral imperative." Repeatedly. As the *Washington Post* recently reported: "For all his claims to support free trade, Bush has yielded to protectionist pressure from a number of special interests."[13] Consider his many violations of his own moral imperative.

- Bush slapped a tariff averaging 39 percent on Canadian softwood lumber—spruce and pine, principally—used primarily in home construction.[14]

  The tariff, which was imposed as part of a trade dispute with Canada in which the U.S. argued that the Canadian government gave its lumber industry unfair subsidies. Three independent panels had ruled against the U.S. before Bush slapped on the tariff. *Tariff* is not a word most Americans use each day, but Bush's tariff on lumber acts as a tax on the American Dream. "This will add nearly $1,500 to the cost of building a typical new home," said Bobby Rayburn, a homebuilder in Jackson, Mississippi.[15]

  Why would Bush violate his moral imperative on lumber? *USA Today* reported that "Analysts say the move was crucial to holding the fast-track vote of Senate Finance Committee Chairman Max Baucus, a Democrat from timber-producing Montana."[16]

- Bush refused to grant Pakistan—our newfound ally in the war on terrorism—the quota relief it had asked for in the area of textiles. *USA Today* said this was because Bush "placated textile interests in North and South Carolina and elsewhere."[17]

- Bush signed a law that barred Vietnamese catfish—or at least a fish the Vietnamese wanted to sell in America as catfish—from being marketed in America as catfish.[18]

- Most telling—and most painful—is steel. Dubya instituted temporary tariffs of up to 30 percent on certain steel imports. Experts say this tariff could better be seen as a tax of 8 to 10 percent on steel—and everything made of steel. *USA Today* described the protectionist move as "the most controversial of the administration's [trade] decisions, it was aimed at extending more help to the troubled U.S. steel industry, which has had various forms of protection on and off for decades. It may also have been *the most nakedly political* of the moves, analysts say, because in addition to shoring up support for fast track, it enhances Bush's reelection prospects in key steel states such as West Virginia, Pennsylvania and Ohio." (Emphasis added.)[19]

"Nakedly political"? How does that square with moral imperative?

I clearly need to brush up on my moral philosophy.

On the campaign trail in 1999, Bush told pro-free-trade farmers where he stood on trade: "I'll work to end tariffs and break down barriers everywhere, entirely, so the whole world trades in freedom. The fearful build walls; the confident demolishes them."[20]

Despite his rhetoric, Bush's actions have landed him squarely among the "fearful." As the insightful economist and *New York Times* columnist Paul Krugman says, "When it comes to free trade, the Bush administration is all for it—unless there is some political cost, however small, to honoring its alleged principles."[21]

Trade is a tough issue. I saw President Clinton catch hell from the best friends Democrats ever had: the men and women of organized labor, over trade. Clinton didn't give fancy lectures about how he was more moral than anyone else because he stood strong for free trade. He simply made the case that, in order to create more high-paying jobs, the United States had to look overseas for markets. And the only way to open the world's markets to our products is to open our markets to the world's.

Rather than try to out-protectionist Bush, Democrats should outsmart him. They should insist that whatever trade agreements he brings to the Congress reflect American—and humanistic—values of respect for the rights of workers and protection for the environment.

If we really want to help the domestic steel industry, a temporary tax on imported steel is not the way to go. Domestic steel would be a lot better off if, instead of taxing consumers in order to buy steel-state votes, Bush would agree to have the federal government absorb the health-care costs of the domestic steel industry. Our competitors in Europe and Japan don't have to pay their retirees' health benefits—society does. But our steel companies are saddled with enormous health-care costs for their retirees, which prices them out of the market.

The Democratic Party must always be the party of the working man and woman. We must never allow George W. Bush to get away with pious lectures about the morality of free trade, then hypocritically slapping protectionist tariffs (that is, taxes) on American consumers. We should stand for a strong and sensible and consistent trade policy.

Investing in People

The damage George W. Bush is doing to our economy and our society by underfunding education, job training, health care, police and other priorities is both real and long term.

He's not cutting those important programs because his dream in life is to leave America poorer, more ignorant and less secure. He's shortchanging our future because his tax cuts have made us short on cash. That $11.54 a week you're getting from the Bush tax cut (if you make between $27,000 and $44,000 a year)[22]—would you trade it for schools in which kids can learn without dodging plaster falling from the ceiling?

Or for continuing President Clinton's COPS program, which put 100,000 new cops on the street—and which Bush is cutting?[23] Or for a prescription drug program for Medicare that will save lives and save money in the long run (by treating diseases with drug therapies rather than surgery or hospitalization)? Or for the peace of mind in knowing that paying for your children's college is within your reach?

Here's the beauty part: Your $11.54 per week doesn't threaten those important investments. As we've seen, the part of the Bush tax cut that helps the middle class has largely already been enacted, and leaving it in place will not explode the deficit. In fact, the nonpartisan Citizens for Tax Justice estimates that freezing the Bush tax cuts would mean middle-class families (between $27,000 and $44,000 in annual income) would only have to forgo $3.62 per week.[24]

However, the $1,021 per week the top 1 percent will get once all of Junior's tax cuts are in place—now that's a different story.[25] That's real money. Money that will make it impossible for us to afford the best education, prescription-drug benefits or law enforcement investments.

Despite the loss of much of their $1,021 a week, even the very wealthiest people will be better off if we continue to make the investments President Clinton began. A skilled workforce, safer communities, better health care and, most of all, a growing economy and a balanced budget—they make America stronger, smarter, safer. The kind of place where lasting prosperity can be built.

The Bottom Line

The good news is that if we freeze the Bush tax cuts we can save Social Security, cut taxes on working people to generate jobs and still have billions left to extend the circle of opportunity to our fellow Americans.

The bad news is that Bush will never, ever freeze his tax cuts for the rich. Because, unlike his dad, who sensibly abandoned his untenable and dishonest tax pledge, Junior will always put his political interests ahead of the national interest.

The best news is we can vote him out of office and replace him with a president who will put economic strength first; a president who will put fiscal sanity first; a president who will put sensible trade policies first; a president who will, to recall a phrase, put people first.

Notes

CHAPTER ONE: THE CLINTON ECONOMY: "THE BEST ECONOMY EVER"

1. According to the U.S. Bureau of Labor Statistics, there were 9.6 million unemployed workers in 1992. Available at www.bls.gov.

2. According to the Bureau of Labor Statistics, private-sector employment increased from 89.4 million in January 1989 to 90.8 million in January 1993. During that same period, public-sector employment rose from 17.6 million to 18.7 million. Thus, 45 percent of the total job growth in the first Bush administration was in the public sector. Available at www.bls.gov.

3. Based on data from the Bureau of Labor Statistics available at www.bls.gov.

4. According to the Bureau of Labor Statistics, total nonfarm payroll employment was 91.003 million in January 1981 and 109.502 million in January 1993. Thus, total employment growth was 18.499 million during the twelve years of the Reagan and first Bush administrations—compared to 22.880 million during the eight years of the Clinton administration. Available at www.bls.gov.

5. According to the Bureau of Labor Statistics, total private nonfarm payroll employment was 90.775 million in January 1993 and 111.695 million in January 2001. Thus, total private employment growth was 20.920 million during the Clinton administration, which is 91.4 percent of the 22.880 million total number of jobs created. Available at www.bls.gov.

6. According to the Bureau of the Census, there were 31.822 million people in poverty in 1981 and 31.745 million people in poverty in 1988. Thus, 77,000 people were lifted out of poverty during the Reagan administration. Available at www.census.gov.

7. The official capacity is listed as 80,106. See http://www.mackbrown texasfootball.com/pages/superstadium.html.

8. A change from 31.822 million to 31.745 million represents a 0.24 percent reduction (31.745/31.822)-1=.24%).

9. According to the Bureau of the Census, there were 39.265 million people in poverty in 1993 and 31.054 million people in poverty in 2000. Thus, 8.2 million people were lifted out of poverty during the Clinton administration. Available at www.census.gov.

10. According to the Bureau of the Census, the New York City population was 7.4 million in July 1999. Available at www.census.gov.

11. A change from 39.625 to 31.054 million represents a 21 percent reduction (39.265/31.054)-1=-20.9%).

12. Matthew 26:11.

13. The *New York Times*, 7/6/90.

14. According to the Bureau of the Census, there were 31.528 million people in poverty in 1989 and 38.014 million people in poverty in 1992. Thus, 6.5 million people were *pushed into* poverty during the first Bush administration. Available at www.census.gov.

15. *See* http://www.census.gov/hhes/poverty/histpov/hstpov2.html.

16. *See* http://www.census.gov/hhes/poverty/histpov/hstpov3.html.

17. *See* http://www.census.gov/hhes/poverty/histpov/hstpov3.html.

18. *See* http://www.census.gov/hhes/poverty/histpov/hstpov3.html.

19. *See* http://www.census.gov/hhes/poverty/histpov/hstpov3.html.

20. *See* http://www.census.gov/hhes/income/histinc/f07.html.

21. During the Reagan-Bush years, typical family income—adjusted for inflation—rose by $3,404. See http://www.census.gov/hhes/income/histinc/f07.html.

22. Sperling, *Bloomberg News* column, 10/5/01.

23. *See* http://www.census.gov/hhes/income/histinc/f03.html.

24. *See* http://www.census.gov/hhes/income/histinc/f03.html.

25. *See* http://www.census.gov/hhes/income/histinc/f06b.html.

26. *See* http://www.census.gov/hhes/income/histinc/f03b.html.

27. *See* http://www.census.gov/hhes/income/histinc/f03c.html.

28. Luke 12:48.

29. *See* Office of Management and Budget, Historical Tables: Budget of the United States Government, Table 1.1 available at http://www.whitehouse.gov/omb/budget/fy2003/pdf/hist.pdf.

30. *See* Congressional Budget Office, Economic and Budget Outlook, 1/93.

31. *Financial Times*, 1/26/93.

32. National Economic Council, 1/01.

33. *See* http://www.bea.doc.gov/.

34. "NCRC Applauds Treasury Study on CRA and Asks for Follow-Up Studies Involving Community Organizations," National Community Reinvestment Coalition Press Release, 4/19/00.

35. Republican Press Conference, 8/5/93.

36. *Congressional Record,* 3/18/93.

37. *Congressional Record,* 8/6/93.

38. *Congressional Record,* 3/18/93.

39. *Dallas Morning News,* 4/2/93.

40. *Congressional Record,* 8/5/93.

41. *See* www.bls.gov.

42. *Federal Reserve Bulletin,* 1/00.

CHAPTER TWO: TAX CUTS FOR THE RICH; DEFICITS FOR THE REST

1. Associated Press, 11/15/91.

2. "Governor George W. Bush: A Tax Cut with a Purpose" 12/1/99, available at http://www.taxplanet.com/bushfactsheet.pdf.

3. Congressional Budget Office, *Budget and Economic Outlook: Fiscal Years 2002–2011,* 1/01.

4. *Los Angeles Times,* 7/13/02.

5. Center on Budget and Policy Priorities Fact Sheet, 1/23/02.

6. *Washington Post,* 7/12/02.

7. Center on Budget and Policy Priorities, "Why the Surplus Has Disappeared"—analysis of the latest CBO data, 8/29/02.

8. Ibid.

9. According to the census, there are 73 million families in America. A 2002 X-Type sedan is listed for $28,477 at www.edmunds.com/new/jaguar/index.html.

10. 1993 Dom Perignon—a very good year—listed at $99 per bottle at www.bacchuscellars.com/buy/champagne/domperignon.htm.

11. Beluga listed at $1,375 per pound at Caviar Malossol Russian Beluga Roes via Amazon.com.

12. Grey Poupon listed at $2.99 for an 8-ounce jar at Giant Grocery via peapod.com.

13. Associated Press, 3/12/02; *Washington Post,* 12/4/01.

14. House Budget Committee, Democratic Staff report: "Return to Red Ink: Back to Budget Deficits 2/8/02; CBO, Budget and Economic Out-

look, Fiscal Years 2003–2012, 1/31/02, Summary Table 2; CBO: An Analysis of the President's Budgetary Proposals for 2003, Table 1, 3/6/02 $1.97 trillion figure from House Budget Committee, Democratic Staff, Analysis of OMB Mid-Session Review, 7/16/02.

15. Congressional Budget Office.

16. CTJ Fact Sheet, 5/26/01, http://www.ctj.org/html/gwbfinal.htm; CBO, Cost Estimate of H.R. 1836, Economic Growth and Tax Relief Reconciliation Act of 2001, http://www.cbo.gov.

17. CBPP Fact Sheet, 4/411/02, http://www.cbpp.org/2-11-02taxfact.htm.

18. CBPP Fact Sheet, 8/2/01, http://www.cbpp.org/8-2-01tax.htm.

19. CTJ Fact Sheet, 5/26/01, http://www.ctj.org/html/gwbfinal.htm.

20. CTJ Fact Sheet, 5/26/01, http://www.ctj.org/html/gwbfinal.htm.

21. CTJ Fact Sheet, 5/26/01, http://www.ctj.org/html/gwbfinal.htm.

22. CBPP Fact Sheet, 3/6/01, http://www.cbpp.org/3-6-01tax.htm.

23. CBPP Fact Sheet, 2/15/01, http://www.cbpp.org.

24. Ibid.

25. CBPP Fact Sheet, 2/15/01, http://www.cbpp.org.

26. CBO, Crippen Testimony before the Senate Budget Committee on the Budget and Economic Outlook: Fiscal Years 2003–2012, 1/23/02 (emphasis added).

27. CBPP Fact Sheet, 1/23/02; Crippen Testimony before the Senate Budget Committee, 1/23/02.

28. George W. Bush, remarks at Western Michigan University, 3/27/01, *Public Papers of the President*, emphasis added.

29. *Washington Post*, 2/6/01.

30. Bush remarks at Bob Riley for Governor/Alabama GOP Victory 2002 Luncheon, 7/15/02.

31. Hillary Rodham Clinton, Remarks to the Democratic Leadership Council, 7/29/02; *New York Times*, 7/30/02.

32. *Washington Post*, 5/15/02.

33. $2.12 billion per month x 12 months = $25.44 billion a year x 67 years = $1.704 trillion. The Bush tax cut, according to CBO, will cost $1.7 trillion over ten years. CBO, Cost Estimate of H.R. 1836, Economic Growth and Tax Relief Reconciliation Act of 2001, http://www.cbo.gov.

34. Remarks following discussions with business leaders, *Public Papers of the President*, 10/3/01.

35. *See*, e.g., Bush remarks following meeting with his economic team and members of the Federal Reserve, *ABC News*, 01/07/02.

36. *Federal Document Clearing House Political Transcripts,* 2/27/02.

37. *Chicago Tribune,* 7/14/02.

38. *The New Republic,* 5/13/02.

39. NBC News Transcripts, *Meet the Press,* 6/9/02.

40. *Dallas Morning News,* 1/8/98.

41. Bush speech: Tax Cut with a Purpose, 12/1/99; *CNN Inside Politics,* 12/1/99.

42. *Ft. Worth Star-Telegram,* 12/1/99.

43. Bush speech, 2/5/01.

44. *Los Angeles Times,* 9/28/01.

45. Bush speech, 10/2/01.

46. *Washington Post,* 10/25/01; H.R. 3090, Roll Call Vote #401, 10/24/01, http://thomas.loc.gov.

47. SAP on H.R. 3090, 10/24/01, http://www.whitehouse.gov.

48. CTJ, Corporate Taxpayers and Corporate Freeloaders, 8/85.

49. *Wall Street Journal,* 10/23/01; *Washington Post,* 10/25/01.

50. *New York Times,* 10/25/01; *Wall Street Journal,* 10/23/01; CTJ Fact Sheet, 10/26/01.

51. FEC Info, www.tray.com; Center for Responsive Politics, Opensecrets.org; *Wall Street Journal,* 10/23/01.

52. FEC Info, www.tray.com; Center for Responsive Politics, Opensecrets.org.

53. *Wall Street Journal,* 10/23/01.

54. FEC Info, www.tray.com; Center for Responsive Politics, Opensecrets.org.

55. *Wall Street Journal,* 10/23/01.

56. FEC Info, www.tray.com; Center for Responsive Politics, Opensecrets.org.

57. *Wall Street Journal,* 10/23/01.

58. FEC Info, www.tray.com; Center for Responsive Politics, Opensecrets.org.

59. *Wall Street Journal,* 10/23/01.

60. FEC Info, www.tray.com; Center for Responsive Politics, Opensecrets.org.

61. *Wall Street Journal,* 10/23/01.

62. FEC Info, www.tray.com; Center for Responsive Politics, Opensecrets.org.

63. *Wall Street Journal,* 10/23/01.

64. FEC Info, www.tray.com; Center for Responsive Politics, Opensecrets.org.

65. *Wall Street Journal,* 10/23/01.

66. FEC Info, www.tray.com; Center for Responsive Politics, Opensecrets.org.

67. *Wall Street Journal,* 10/23/01.

68. *Wall Street Journal,* 10/23/01.

69. *Washington Post,* 10/25/01.

70. CTJ Fact Sheet, 10/12/01.

71. CBPP Fact Sheet, 9/20/01.

72. *New York Times,* 9/26/01.

73. *New York Times,* 9/26/01; 10/18/01.

74. CTJ Fact Sheet, 10/5/01.

75. CTJ Fact Sheet, 10/5/01.

76. *Los Angeles Times,* 10/12/01.

77. *Christian Science Monitor,* 10/15/01.

78. Center for Budget and Policy Priorities Study, 2/6/01.

79. Citizens for Tax Justice study, http://www.ctj.org/html/estbob.htm.

80. Ibid.

81. Center for Budget and Policy Priorities study, 2/6/01.

82. Citizens for Tax Justice, http://www.ctj.org/html/estbob.htm.

83. Ibid.

84. Center for Budget and Policy Priorities study, 2/6/01.

85. *Washington Post,* 2/6/01.

CHAPTER THREE: SOCIAL SECURITY: STRAP GRANNY
INTO THE ROLLER COASTER

1. George W. Bush speech: Rancho Cucamonga, California, *Washington Post,* 4/15/00.

2. Bush remarks at National Newspaper Association 40th Annual Government Affairs Conference, 3/22/01; *Federal News Service,* 3/22/01.

3. Associated Press, 3/6/02.

4. *USA Today,* 8/28/01.

5. *Orlando Sentinel,* 2/5/02.

6. *Washington Post,* 5/2/01.

7. *Washington Post,* 5/3/01; *New York Times,* 5/3/01; *Los Angeles Times,* 5/4/01.

8. Terry Moran, *ABC News,* 5/2/01.

9. US Newswire, National Committee to Preserve Social Security and Medicare, 6/11/01 press release.

10. *New York Times,* 5/3/01.

11. Center on Budget and Policy Priorities: *Social Security Reform,* 12/3/01.

12. *Boston Globe,* 11/30/01; *Wall Street Journal,* 11/30/01; Center on Budget and Policy Priorities: *Social Security Reform,* 12/3/01.

13. Center on Budget and Policy Priorities, "Social Security Commission Plans Would Entail Substantial Benefit Reductions and Large Subsidies for Private Accounts," 6/18/02.

14. Source: Tucker Carlson, bull session while we were supposed to be working at CNN's *Crossfire,* 8/14/02.

15. NBC News Transcripts, *Meet the Press,* 11/21/99; *New York Daily News,* 11/24/99.

16. *Wall Street Journal,* 11/30/01.

17. *Business Week,* 5/30/01.

18. *New York Times,* 11/29/01; *USA Today,* 12/4/01; *Washington Post,* 12/4/01; Social Security Commission press conference, 12/11/01; Center on Budget and Policy Priorities, "Social Security Reform: The Questions Raised by the Plans Endorsed by President Bush's Social Security Commission," revised 12/3/01.

19. Governor George W. Bush, St. Charles, Missouri, 11/2/00; *Washington Post,* 11/3/00.

20. *Boston Globe,* editorial, 5/4/01.

21. Center on Budget and Policy Priorities: "Social Security Reform," 12/3/01; Democratic Staff of the Committee on Ways and Means, 11/30/01.

22. Study assumes half of the money in individual accounts would have been placed in the stock market, Center for Economic and Policy Research: "The Stock Market Bubble and Investing Social Security in the Stock Market," 7/22/02; *Wall Street Journal,* 7/23/02.

23. Economic Policy Institute, Snapshot for 1/30/02; Information based on average wage earner beginning work in 1966 at age 30, employed at Enron in 1985 and retired in 2001.

24. Krugman column, *New York Times,* 7/25/02.

25. *Wall Street Journal,* 6/12/01.

26. *Financial Times,* 5/19/01.

27. Center on Budget and Policy Priorities Paper: "Social Security and the Tax Cut; The 75-Year Cost of the Tax Cut Is More Than Twice as Large as the Long-Term Deficit in Social Security." www.cbpp.org/4-9-02socsec.pdf.

CHAPTER FOUR: (DIS)INVESTING IN PEOPLE

1. *Knoxville News-Sentinel,* 2/22/01.

2. *Chicago Sun-Times,* 4/24/01.

3. *Federal News Service,* 4/30/02.

4. *San Antonio Express-News,* 6/31/01.

5. *Weekly Compilation of Presidential Documents,* 4/18/01.

6. *Federal News Service,* 4/9/02.

7. *Chicago Sun-Times,* 1/15/01.

8. Remarks by the president during Leadership Forum, Old Carnegie Library, Council Bluffs, Iowa, 2/28/01, www.whitehouse.gov.

9. Center for Defense Information, World Military Expenditures, http://www.cdi.org/issues/wme/.

10. Ibid.

11. Remarks on signing the No Child Left Behind Act of 2001, *Federal News Service,* 1/8/02, (emphasis added).

12. House Committee on Education and the Workforce, Democratic staff, The Bush Budget: Shortchanging School Reform, 2/12/02 (emphasis added).

13. Kennedy Press Release, 2/12/02.

14. Democratic staffs of the Committee on Education and the Workforce of the U.S. House of Representatives and the Committee on Health, Education, Labor, and Pensions of the U.S. Senate, 2/12/02.

15. Committee on Budget, Democratic Staff, *Summary and Analysis of the President's 2003 Budget,* 2/8/02.

16. House Democratic staff of the Committee on Education and the Workforce, 2/5/02.

17. President Bush, 1/29/02; Democratic staffs of the Committee on Education and the Workforce of the U.S. House of Representatives and the Committee on Health, Education, Labor, and Pensions of the U.S. Senate, 2/12/02.

18. House Democratic staff of the Committee on Education and the Workforce, 2/5/02.

19. House Democratic Staff of the Committee on Education and the Workforce, 2/5/02.

20. National Center for Education Statistics, *How Old Are America's Public Schools?*, 1/99, www.nces.ed.gov; GAO Report, *School Facilities*, 3/00; American Institute of Architects, *Good Enough for Congress?*; www.e-architect.com; House Democratic Staff of the Committee on Education and the Workforce, 2/5/02.

21. Democratic staffs of the Committee on Education and the Workforce of the U.S. House of Representatives and the Committee on Health, Education, Labor, and Pensions of the U.S. Senate, 2/12/02.

22. 6/15/00 Bush interview; *Business Week*, 6/21/00.

23. *Atlanta Journal and Constitution*, 4/10/01; *Washington Post*, 5/10/01; AP, 4/18/01; internal calculations, Senator Pat Roberts Press Conference, 3/6/01.

24. *CQ Monitor News*, 5/3/01; Associated Press, 5/4/01; S1, 5/3/01, Harkin-Hagel Amndt Voice Vote.

25. *Washington Post*, 5/10/01.

26. President Bush, 1/19/02; Democratic staffs of the Committee on Education and the Workforce of the U.S. House of Representatives and the Committee on Health, Education, Labor, and Pensions of the U.S. Senate, 2/12/02.

27. Democratic staffs of the Committee on Education and the Workforce of the U.S. House of Representatives and the Committee on Health, Education, Labor, and Pensions of the U.S. Senate, 2/12/02.

28. *CQ Monitor News*, 5/2/01; House Appropriations Committee, Democratic Staff: *Bush Administration Budget Proposals Affecting Labor-HHS-Education Appropriations*, Revised 5/15/01; Department of Education FY2002 Justifications of Appropriations Estimates to the Congress, Volume 1; www.ed.gov.

29. *CQ Monitor News*, 5/2/01, 5/3/01; S1, 5/3/01, CQ #91.

30. *CQ Monitor News*, 5/3/01.

31. Democratic staffs of the Committee on Education and the Workforce of the U.S. House of Representatives and the Committee on Health, Education, Labor, and Pensions of the U.S. Senate, 2/12/02.

32. Ibid.

33. *Houston Post,* 1/5/95.

34. www.nea.org.

35. Democratic staffs of the Committee on Education and the Workforce of the U.S. House of Representatives and the Committee on Health, Education, Labor, and Pensions of the U.S. Senate, 2/12/02.

36. Democratic Education and Workforce Committee, *Building a Future for America's Minority-Serving Institutions,* 3/22/01.

37. Democratic Education and Workforce Committee, *Building a Future for America's Minority-Serving Institutions,* 3/22/01; College Board, *College Costs Increase but Record Amount of Financial Aid Is Available to Students,* www.collegeboard.com.

38. Associated Press, 8/30/00; www.ed.gov.

39. *New York Times,* 2/1/02; House Democratic Staff of the Committee on Education and the Workforce, 2/5/02; Democratic Policy Committee, Bush Budget and Education, 5/3/01.

40. Associated Press, 2/11/02; House Democratic Staff of the Committee on Education and the Workforce, 2/5/02.

41. www.ed.gov.

42. *New York Times,* 4/28/02.

43. *Washington Post,* 4/30/02.

44. House Committee on Education and Workforce, Democratic Staff, The State Budget Crisis and Higher Education.

45. *New York Times,* 2/4/02; *CQ Monitor News,* 2/5/02.

46. *Washington Times,* 2/5/02.

47. *CQ Monitor News,* 2/5/02; U.S. Conference of Mayors Press Release, 2/4/02; Department of Labor Press Release, 6/28/01.

48. Department of Labor Press Release, 2/7/02; AFL-CIO, "Cuts that Hurt: The Bush FY2003 Budget for Workers and Their Families," 2/02; Bush FY2003 Budget, 2/4/02.

49. House Education and the Workforce Committee Hearing, 10/16/01; AFL-CIO, "Cuts that Hurt: The Bush FY2003 Budget for Workers and Their Families," 2/02.

50. Department of Labor, "Budget Overview FY2003—Agency Information," 2/4/02; Department of Labor, "Training and Employment Guidance Letter No. 12-00," 3/6/01.

51. *Legal Times,* 2/11/02.

52. *Legal Times,* 2/11/02.

53. *Albuquerque Tribune*, 4/29/02 (emphasis added).

54. Associated Press, 2/4/02.

55. Bush remarks on Trade and Agriculture, 4/24/02; Bush remarks at South Dakota Republican Party Victory 2002 Rally, 4/24/02.

56. Associated Press, 4/22/02; Johnson Letter to Bush, 4/22/02; USDA Bioenergy Program, http://www.fsa.usda.gov/daco/bio_daco.htm, Participant Payments FY2001; Program Participants.

57. Remarks at the University of Pittsburgh Medical Center, 2/5/02.

58. HHS, FY2003 Budget in Brief, http://www.hhs.gov/budget/docbudget.htm.

59. United Press International, 4/3/01; Bush remarks in Wilmington, DE, 4/3/01.

60. White House Press Release, 4/9/01; *Washington Post*, 4/12/01.

61. Bush remarks at Leadership Forum in Atlanta, 3/1/01; *Atlanta Journal and Constitution*, 3/2/01 (emphasis added).

62. HRSA Overview, HHS FY2002 Budget Request, http://www.hhs.gov/budget/docbudget.htm; HRSA Press Release, 10/5/00, http://newsroom.hrsa.gov.

63. Ibid.

CHAPTER FIVE: THE BEST ENVIRONMENT MONEY CAN BUY

1. *Washington Post*, 4/24/01.

2. *Dallas Morning News*, 3/30/01.

3. *Seattle Post-Intelligencer*, 3/28/01.

4. Environmental News Network, 4/24/01, http://www.enn.com/enn-news-archive/2001/04/04242001/finance_43155.asp.

5. Bush speech, "A Comprehensive National Energy Policy," 9/29/00, Saginaw, MI (emphasis added).

6. Associated Press, 3/13/01; *Washington Post*, 3/14/01; Bush letter to Senator Chuck Hagel, 3/13/01.

7. Associated Press, 5/23/00.

8. *Las Vegas Review-Journal*, 10/25/00.

9. www.fec.gov.

10. *Washington Post*, 1/11/02; 11/30/01; *New York Times*, 2/15/02; 2/16/02.

11. *Atlanta Journal-Constitution*, 1/26/02; Citizen Alert, Factsheet, "Top Ten Reasons Why Yucca Mountain Is a Bad Place for Nuclear Waste."

12. Safe Energy Communication Council press release, 5/16/01.

13. *New York Times*, 2/24/02.

14. *New York Times*, 2/24/02.

15. *Boston Globe*, 3/21/01.

16. Environmental Protection Agency Office of Water, "Technical Fact Sheet: Proposed Rule for Arsenic in Drinking Water and Clarifications to Compliance and New Source Contaminants Monitoring (EPA 815-F-00-011) 5/00.

17. Environmental News Network, 4/24/01, http://www.enn.com/enn-news-archive/2001/04/04242001/finance_43155.asp.

18. Ibid.

19. Natural Resources Defense Council Study: "Rewriting the Rules: The Bush Administration's Assault on the Environment," 4/22/02.

20. Ibid.

21. *Washington Post*, 8/8/01, 3/18/02; Bush Energy Plan, Appendix, May 2001; *New York Times*, 1/8/02.

22. *Washington Post*, 6/14/02.

23. *Washington Post*, 6/14/02.

24. *Washington Post*, 6/14/02.

25. Schaeffer, Eric, "Clearing the Air: Why I Quit Bush's EPA," *Washington Monthly*, July/August 2002.

26. Letter from Eric Schaeffer to Christine Todd Whitman, 3/2/02.

27. Ibid.

28. Ibid.

29. Ibid.

30. Schaeffer, Eric, "Clearing the Air: Why I Quit Bush's EPA", *Washington Monthly*, July/August, 2002.

31. American Lung Association press release, 6/13/02, www.lungusa.org/press/envir/air 061402.html.

32. *The Tonight Show with Jay Leno*, NBC, 6/20/02.

33. *The Tonight Show with Jay Leno*, NBC, 6/17/02.

34. Bush press conference in Canton, OH, 6/16/00; Associated Press, 3/29/01; *Denver Post*, 3/15/01.

35. *New York Times*, 1/31/02.

36. *Time*, 8/13/01.

37. CBS News, 4/18/02, http://www.cbsnews.com/stories/2002/03/04/politics/main502844.shtml.

38. National Center for Public Policy Research, a pro-ANWR drilling group. 1/23/02, http://www.nationalcenter.org/TSR12302.html.

39. American Council for an Energy-Efficient Economy, 5/1/01.

40. CNN 4/12/02; http://www.cnn.com/2002/ALLPOLITICS/04/11/anwr.senate.

41. *Denver Post*, 4/21/02.

42. *Seattle Post-Intelligencer*, 3/31/02.

43. *Deseret News*, 5/13/97.

44. *New York Times*, 8/16/01.

45. *Los Angeles Times*, 3/22/01.

46. *Inter Press Service*, 3/22/01.

47. *Los Angeles Times*, 3/22/01.

48. *New York Times*, 8/16/01.

49. Ibid.

50. *San Francisco Chronicle*, 12/28/01.

51. *USA Today*, 6/14/02.

52. *Washington Post*, 1/15/01.

53. *USA Today*, 6/14/02.

54. *Washington Post*, 5/10/01.

55. *Washington Post*, 8/9/01.

56. Natural Resources Defense Council Study: The Bush-Cheney Energy Plan—Players, Profits and Paybacks, 6/01.

57. *Washington Post*, 4/16/01.

58. *Newsweek*, 5/14/01.

59. Natural Resources Defense Council Study: The Bush-Cheney Energy Plan—Players, Profits and Paybacks, 6/01, citing www.opensecrets.org.

60. Associated Press, 5/31/01.

61. Center for Public Integrity, Special Report: "Large GOP Contributor Participated in Secret Energy Task Force Meetings," 1/31/02; updated 3/4/02.

62. *New York Times*, 3/1/02.

63. Natural Resources Defense Council Study: The Bush-Cheney Energy Plan—Players, Profits and Paybacks, 6/01.

CHAPTER SIX: CRIME IN THE SUITES: HOW THE REPUBLICANS
TOLD CORPORATE AMERICA "ANYTHING GOES"

1. *Wall Street Journal,* 3/3/95.

2. *Congressional Record,* 100th Congress, First Session, 6/26/87.

3. David Maraniss and Michael Weisskopf, *Tell Newt to Shut Up!* p. 12, Touchstone Books, Simon & Schuster, New York, 1996.

4. CNN, *Money Line,* 6/28/02.

5. *Nightline,* ABC News, 7/18/02.

6. www.opensecrets.org.

7. http://www.infoplease.com/ipa/A0760610.html.

8. Ibid.

9. U.S. Fish & Wildlife Service, http://www.fws.gov/r9extaff/eaglejuly2.html.

10. Ibid.

11. Ibid.

12. Jan Reid, *Mother Jones,* September/October 1996.

13. http://motlc.wiesenthal.com/pages/t025/t02549.html.

14. *Wall Street Journal,* 3/3/95.

15. *Washington Post,* 3/12/95.

16. Jan Reid, *Mother Jones,* September/October 1996.

17. *Washington Post,* 3/12/95.

18. Ibid.

19. U.S. Capitol Historical Society; http://www.uschs.org/Exhibit/heresirpeoplegovern.htm.

20. *Washington Post,* 3/12/95.

21. Ibid.

22. *Newsday,* 8/23/95.

23. *Washington Post,* 9/24/95.

24. 12/20/95 veto message of the President of the United States.

25. *Legal Times,* 4/8/02.

26. PBS *Frontline,* 6/20/02.

27. *Chicago Tribune,* 12/21/00.

28. *Insights,* 10/98.

29. *Business Week,* 9/25/00.

30. *Cleveland Plain Dealer,* 10/2/00.

31. *Business Week,* 9/25/00.

32. *New Republic,* 2/11/02.

33. *Business Week,* 9/25/00.

34. *Washington Post,* 1/25/02.

35. PBS "Frontline," 6/20/02.

36. *Wall Street Journal,* 10/25/00.

37. *New Yorker,* 4/22/02.

38. Salon.com, 7/4/02.

39. *The New Republic,* 7/22/02.

40. *Business Week,* 9/25/00.

41. *Time,* 2/4/02.

42. House Democratic Policy Committee, 7/11/02.

43. Ibid.

44. GAO Report, GAO-02-302, 3/5/02.

45. *Wall Street Journal,* 2/28/00; *American Banker,* 2/29/00; *New York Law Journal,* 4/28/00.

46. *New York Law Journal,* 2/15/01; *Newsday,* 7/1/01; *New York Times,* 8/19/01; *Washington Post,* 1/16/02.

47. House Democratic Policy Committee, 7/11/02.

48. *Wall Street Journal,* 12/13/01.

49. *USA Today,* 1/24/02.

50. Public Citizen, 12/01.

51. *American Prospect,* 2/25/02.

52. *Dallas Morning News,* 3/10/02.

53. *New York Times,* 1/20/02.

54. House Democratic Policy Committee, 7/12/02.

55. Ibid.

56. Statement of Paul H. O'Neill before the Senate Committee on Governmental Affairs, Permanent Subcommittee on Investigations: OECD Harmful Tax Practices Initiative, 7/18/01.

57. Statement of Robert Morgenthau to the Senate Permanent Subcommittee on Investigations, 7/18/01.

58. *New York Times,* 9/20/01.

59. *American Prospect,* 10/22/01.

60. *New York Times,* 9/20/01.

61. *Plan Sponsor,* 9/98; online at http://www.assetpub.com/ archive/ps/98-08pssept/sept98PS26.html.

62. House Democratic Policy Committee, 7/11/02.

63. CNN 3/20/01, http://www.cnn.com/2001/ALLPOLITICS/03/20/ bush.ergonomics/.

64. *Financial Times* (London), 6/14/02.

65. Ibid.

66. *Washington Post,* 7/10/02.

67. *Los Angeles Times,* 8/12/02.

68. *National Journal's Congress Daily,* 3/21/02; CNN, Market Call, 6/27/02; ABC News *This Week,* 6/30/02.

69. *National Post* (Canada), 7/18/02.

70. *CQ Weekly,* 5/25/02; 7/27/02; CNN, Lou Dobbs *Moneyline,* 6/28/02.

71. *Washington Post,* 7/13/02.

72. Ibid.

73. Ibid.

74. Ibid.

75. Ibid.

76. *Atlanta Journal-Constitution,* 6/20/02.

77. United Press International, 12/20/95.

CHAPTER SEVEN: BUSH, INC.:
A WHOLLY OWNED SUBSIDIARY OF ENRON

1. *USA Today,* 11/30/01; *Texas State Archives,* "1995 Texas Inaugural Committee"; "1999 Texas Inaugural Committee."

2. *San Diego Union-Tribune,* 2/11/01; *Atlanta Journal-Constitution,* 4/27/00; Center for Responsive Politics, www.crp.org; Political Money Line, www.tray.com.

3. http://www.opensecrets.org/alerts/v5/alertv5_37a.asp; *Washington Post,* 7/27/02.

4. Center for Responsive Politics, www.crp.org.

5. *New York Times,* 3/6/02.

6. Ibid.

7. *The Nation,* 11/21/94.

8. Ibid.

9. Ibid.

10. Ibid.

11. Ibid.

12. Ibid.

13. Ibid., and *Texas Observer,* 11/11/94.

14. Ibid.

15. Ibid.

16. Ibid.

17. Correspondence is online at www.thedailyenron.com/documents.

18. *New York Times,* 6/30/00.

19. *Dallas Morning News,* 2/16/02.

20. *Philadelphia Daily News,* 2/1/02.

21. Sierra Club Press Release, 6/1/99; *San Antonio Express-News,* 6/4/99; Texans for Public Justice report: "Dirty Air, Dirty Money," June 1998; Center for Responsive Politics; *Grandfathered Air Pollution: The Dirty Secret of Texas Industries,* 4/27/98.

22. "The Road to the Presidency, a Timeline of the 2000 Presidential Campaign," Kennedy School of Government, Harvard University, 2/24/01.

23. Associated Press, *Detroit News,* 4/8/00.

24. *The Daily Enron.*

25. *US News & World Report,* 6/18/01.

26. Ibid.

27. *New York Times,* 6/3/01.

28. Associated Press, 6/20/01; 6/27/01.

29. Letter from Sens. Carl Levin and John Warner to Secretary of the Army Thomas White, 3/1/02, http://www.senate.gov/~levin/releases/levin.pdf.

30. *Seattle Post-Intelligencer,* 7/19/02.

31. *Press Trust of India,* 7/21/01; *Baltimore Sun,* 1/12/01.

32. *Washington Post,* 1/18/02.

33. Ibid.

34. "The Public I," Center for Public Integrity, 1/11/02.

35. Ibid.

36. ABC News, 12/10/01; http://abcnews.go.com/sections/politics/DailyNews/enron011210.html.

37. Associated Press, 2/1/02.

38. *New York Times,* 5/25/01.

39. Ibid.

40. *New York Times,* 5/25/01.

41. Ibid.

42. CNN, 2/9/02; http://www.cnn.com/2002/ALLPOLITICS/02/09/enron.ferc/.

43. Associated Press, 2/23/02.

44. Ibid.

45. Minority Staff, Committee on Government Reform, U.S. House of Representatives, "How the White House Energy Plan Benefited Enron," 1/16/02.

46. Ibid., 2.

47. Ibid., 4.

48. Ibid., 5–6.

49. Ibid., 6–7.

50. Ibid., 7–8.

51. Ibid., 9.

52. Ibid., 9–10.

53. Ibid., 11–12.

54. Ibid., 12.

55. Ibid., 13–14.

56. Ibid., 14–15.

57. Ibid., 15–16.

58. Ibid., 16–17.

59. Ibid., 18.

60. Ibid., 18–19.

61. Ibid., 19–20.

62. Ibid., 20.

63. *Financial Times,* 2/9/02.

64. *New York Times,* 5/25/01.

65. Letter from David S. Addington, Counsel to the Vice President, to Rep. Henry A. Waxman, 1/3/02.

CHAPTER EIGHT: TAKING CARE OF BIDNESS: BUSH AND HARKEN ENERGY

1. *Washington Post*, 7/30/99.

2. *Washington Post*, 7/30/99.

3. *New York Times*, 3/6/02.

4. *The Nation*, 7/17/02.

5. *Public Papers of the President*, 7/8/02.

6. *Los Angeles Times*, 7/12/02.

7. *Wall Street Journal*, 7/11/02.

8. *Public Papers of the President*, 7/8/02.

9. *New York Times*, 7/20/02.

10. *New York Daily News*, 2/19/00.

11. *New York Times*, 3/6/02.

12. Molly Ivins and Louis Dubose, *Mother Jones*, March/April 2000.

13. *Dallas Morning News*, 7/30/99.

14. *The Nation*, 7/17/02.

15. Ivins and Dubose, *Mother Jones*, March/April 2000, citing *Time* magazine, 1991.

16. *Los Angeles Times*, 7/12/02.

17. Ibid.

18. Ibid.

19. Ibid.

20. Center for Public Integrity, 4/4/00.

21. *Los Angeles Times*, 7/12/02.

22. Official Transcript, Presidential press conference, The White House, 7/8/02, http://www.whitehouse.gov/news/releases/2002/07/20020708-5.html.

23. Official Transcript, Presidential press conference, The White House, 7/8/02, http://www.whitehouse.gov/news/releases/2002/07/20020708-5.html.

24. *Washington Post*, 7/11/02.

25. *Los Angeles Times*, 7/12/02.

26. Econstats, on the web at http://www.econstats.com/r_aal.htm.

27. Harken Energy Corp., Form 10-K, 1989.

28. The Daily Enron, http://www.thedailyenron.com/documents/
20020307061926-97282.asp.

29. Associated Press, 7/16/02.

30. Ibid.

31. Ibid.

32. *New York Daily News*, 7/31/02.

33. *Washington Post*, 8/1/02.

34. *Wall Street Journal*, 8/1/02.

35. Ibid.

36. Ibid.

37. Securities and Exchange Commission, Division of Enforcement,
http://www.sec.gov/divisions/enforce/insider.htm.

38. Ibid.

39. *Dallas Morning News*, 10/11/94; *Time*, 10/28/91; *Wall Street Journal*,
12/6/91.

40. Center for Public Integrity, 4/4/00.

41. *Dallas Morning News*, 10/11/94.

42. *Dallas Morning News*, 5/7/94.

43. *Dallas Morning News*, 10/11/94.

44. *Dallas Morning News*, 10/11/94.

45. Associated Press, 9/6/00.

46. Harken Energy Corporation, "Analysis of Cash Needs," 5/4/90;
Dallas Morning News, 10/11/94.

47. Securities and Exchange Commission, Memorandum, 4/9/91.

48. *Dallas Morning News*, 5/7/94.

49. *Houston Chronicle*, 5/8/94.

50. *Time*, 10/28/91.

51. *Austin American-Statesman*, 10/9/94; www.whitehouse.gov, 7/3/02;
Bush Press Conference, 7/8/02.

52. *Wall Street Journal*, 7/11/02.

53. *Dallas Morning News*, 10/11/94.

54. *Washington Post*, 7/30/99.

55. *Washington Post*, 1/18/89; *Legal Times*, 12/5/88.

56. *Financial Times* (London), 6/1/92; *USA Today,* 2/27/92.

57. *USA Today,* 2/27/92.

58. *Houston Chronicle,* 10/13/94; Associated Press, 9/6/00; *American Lawyer,* 11/89.

59. *Washington Post,* 7/4/02.

60. *Houston Chronicle,* 10/13/94.

61. *Washington Post,* 7/11/02.

62. *Washington Post,* 7/30/99.

CHAPTER NINE: HALLIBURTON: HOW DICK CHENEY PUT
THE "VICE" IN VICE PRESIDENT

1. *Wall Street Journal,* 5/10/02.

2. CNN, 7/26/00.

3. http://www.whitehouse.gov/vicepresident/vpbio.html.

4. http://www.quotationspage.com/subjects/honor.

5. *New York Times,* 5/30/02.

6. *New York Times,* 5/22/02.

7. Ibid.

8. *New York Times,* 5/22/02.

9. Halliburton Press Release, "Halliburton Reports SEC Investigation of Accounting Practice," 5/28/02.

10. *Wall Street Journal,* 5/10/02.

11. *Newsweek,* 7/22/02.

12. *USA Today,* 7/25/00.

13. Ibid.

14. Ibid.

15. http://www.whitehouse.gov/vicepresident/vpbio.html.

16. Halliburton Proxy Statement, 4/5/99.

17. Halliburton Co., 10-K, 12/31/98.

18. The White House: "Specifics on the President's Ten-Point Plan," 3/7/02.

19. The White House: "Specifics on the President's Ten-Point Plan," 3/7/02.

20. Halliburton proxies filed 4/2/97, 4/5/99, 4/3/00, 4/2/01.

21. "Specifics on the President's Ten-Point Plan," 3/7/02.

22. Remarks by President Bush and President Kwasniewski of Poland in Press Conference, 7/17/02; *Baltimore Sun*, 7/18/02.

23. *Newsweek*, 7/22/02.

24. *Newsweek*, 7/22/02.

25. *New York Times*, 5/22/02.

26. Associated Press, 8/17/00.

27. *USA Today*, 7/25/00.

28. *New York Times*, 8/12/00.

29. *Austin Chronicle*, 6/7/02.

30. *New York Times*, 8/26/00.

31. ABC News, *This Week*, 7/30/00.

32. ABC News, *This Week*, 8/27/00.

33. ABC News, *This Week*, 8/27/00.

34. *Washington Post*, 6/23/01.

35. Ibid.

36. Ibid.

37. Ibid.

38. *New York Times*, 8/24/00.

39. *Wall Street Journal*, 2/1/01; State Department, "Patterns of Global Terrorism: 1999," www.state.gov/www/global/terrorism/1999report/intro.html.

40. Hart's Middle East Oil and Gas, 6/27/00.

41. CNN, *Inside Politics*, 7/26/00; State Department, "Patterns of Global Terrorism: 1999, www.state.gov/www/global/terrorism/1999report/intro.html.

42. ABC, *World News This Morning*, 7/30/00.

43. UPI, 7/31/00.

44. *Amarillo Globe-News*, 6/13/98.

45. Both numbers were cited in the *Washington Post*, 8/1/02.

46. www.Salon.com, 8/1/02.

47. Ibid., citing Citizen Works study (As corrected—it originally had overstated the number of years Halliburton had paid no taxes. Two years is correct).

CHAPTER TEN: THE KEYSTONE KOPS: BUSH AND HIS ECONOMIC TEAM

1. *Public Papers of the President*, 4/21/01.

2. CNN Live Event, 1/4/01.

3. *Washington Post*, 8/1/02.

4. *Wall Street Journal*, quoted in the *New Republic*, 8/5/02, 8/12/02.

5. The Baseball Page, http://www.thebaseballpage.com/features/mets_debut.htm.

6. *New York Times*, 8/12/02.

7. *Washington Post*, 9/10/02: "Bush aides had hoped for a stock market rally after his 27-minute speech at the Regent Wall Street hotel."

8. *New York Times*, 8/12/02.

9. Ibid.

10. Ibid.

11. Ibid.

12. *Los Angeles Times*, 8/12/02.

13. *New York Times*, 8/12/02.

14. *New York Times*, 8/14/02.

15. Ibid.

16. Ibid.

17. *Washington Times*, 8/13/02.

18. *New York Times*, 8/14/02.

19. Ibid.

20. Ibid.

21. www.liberaloasis.com.

22. Ibid.

23. *Washington Times*, 10/22/01.

24. *Fortune*, 9/2/02.

25. *Texas Observer, Bushfiles*, citing *Fortune* magazine, April 1999; http://www.bushfiles.com/bushfiles/manufacture.html.

26. *Fortune*, 9/2/02.

27. *New York Times*, 11/1/01 (emphasis added).

28. AFL-CIO, Layoff Tracker, http://www.aflcio.org; BLS, Employment Situation Summary, 11/2/01; http://www.bls.gov; *Wall Street Journal*, 11/2/01.

29. ABC Radio, 1/15/02.

30. *New York Times,* quoted in the *New Republic,* 8/5/02, 8/12/02.

31. *Financial Times,* 5/19/01.

32. *Newsweek,* 3/26/01.

33. Paul O'Neill testimony before Senate Banking Committee, 1/17/01.

34. Bush Exchange with Reporters in Portland, ME, 3/23/01.

35. *Washington Times,* 3/22/01.

36. *New York Times,* 10/16/01.

37. *Washington Post,* 10/17/01.

38. *Washington Post,* 8/1/02.

39. Ibid.

40. Ibid.

41. *New York Times,* 8/12/02.

42. Ibid.

43. *Time,* 7/29/02.

44. http://www.mdle.com/ClassicFilms/FeaturedStar/keystone.htm.

45. *Washington Post,* 10/7/01.

46. *Los Angeles Times,* 10/17/01.

47. *New York Times,* 10/2/01.

48. *Washington Post,* 11/28/01.

49. President George W. Bush, Remarks to *Farmers Journal* Cooperative Convention, 11/28/01.

50. *Nightly Business Report,* PBS, 11/9/01.

51. Vice President Richard Cheney, Remarks to the U.S. Chamber of Commerce, 11/14/01.

52. O'Neill Media Availability, 11/16/01.

53. CNN, *Novak, Hunt & Shields,* 10/6/01.

54. *Washington Post,* 10/15/01.

55. Pitt PFD Form, filed 7/10/01.

56. *Los Angeles Times,* editorial, 12/9/01.

57. Remarks before the AICPA Governing Council by Chairman Harvey L. Pitt, U.S. Securities & Exchange Commission, Miami Beach, Florida, October 22, 2001. See full text at http://www.sec.gov/news/speech/spch516.htm.

58. Ibid.

59. Ibid.

60. *Wall Street Journal*, 1/30/02.

61. *New York Times*, 5/15/02.

62. *New York Times, Wall Street Journal*, 5/15/02.

63. *New York Times*, 5/15/02.

64. Reuters, 5/6/02.

65. Ibid.

66. Ibid.

67. CNN, 7/24/02.

CHAPTER ELEVEN: WHAT THE DEMOCRATS ARE FOR (OR AT LEAST WHAT THEY SHOULD BE FOR)

1. Citizens for Tax Justice, http://www.ctj.org/html/gwbfinal.htm.

2. *Washington Post*, 7/21/02.

3. Center on Budget and Policy Priorities Paper: "Social Security and the Tax Cut; The 75-Year Cost of the Tax Cut Is More Than Twice as Large as the Long-Term Deficit in Social Security." www.cbpp.org/4-9-02socsec.pdf.

4. *Washington Post*, 2/6/01.

5. www.cbpp.org/5-25-00tax.htm.

6. *Boston Globe*, 4/15/01.

7. Ibid.

8. Ibid.

9. President George W. Bush, Address to the Council of the Americas, *Public Papers of the President*, 5/7/01.

10. Kant, Immanuel, *Grounding of the Metaphysics of Morals.*

11. Ibid.

12. In this discussion I am indebted to three essays on Kant: "Kant's Moral Axioms" by Marian Hillar, on the web at www.socinian.org/kant.html#_edn2; "Kant's Moral Theory" (author not cited) on the web at www.cs.cca.ccoes.edu/phill 12/kant.htm; and "Kant: The Ethical Imperative: The Good Will and Respect For Others" by Gordon L. Ziniewicz on the web at http://www.fred.net/tzaka/kant2.html.

13. *Washington Post*, 7/28/02.

14. *BBC News*, 3/22/02, www.news.bbc.co.uk.

15. Ibid.

16. *USA Today*, 5/2/02.

17. Ibid.

18. Ibid.

19. Ibid. (emphasis added).

20. Remarks at a Republican fund-raiser in Iowa, 6/12/99, Federal Document Clearinghouse Documents Political Transcripts.

21. *New York Times,* 6/11/02.

22. CTJ Fact Sheet, 5/26/01, http://www.ctj.org/html/gwbfinal.htm.

23. *Newsday,* 6/10/02.

24. Citizens for Tax Justice, www.ctj.org/html/gwb0402.htm.

25. CTJ Fact Sheet, 5/26/01, http://www.ctj.org/html/gwbfinal.htm.